Low Carb Low Cholesterol Cookbook for Beginners

The Complete Anti-inflammatory Solutions and Recipes for A Healthy You

Dr.Nia Burke

TABLE OF CONTENTS

Introduction

Sarah found herself sitting in a doctor's office, her mind swirling with worry and confusion. The doctor had just delivered news that shook her to her core: her cholesterol levels were alarmingly high, putting her at risk for serious health complications. As Sarah left the office, a flood of questions filled her mind. How had this happened? What could she do to improve her health and lower her cholesterol? Little did she know, this moment would mark the beginning of a transformative journey toward better health through the power of low carb, anti-inflammatory cooking.

Understanding Low Carb and Cholesterol: Debunking Myths and Facts

In recent years, low carb diets have gained widespread popularity as a means of weight loss and improving overall health. However, there is often confusion surrounding the relationship between low carb diets and cholesterol levels. In this section, we'll delve into the myths and facts surrounding low carb and cholesterol, providing you with a clear understanding of how these two factors intersect and influence each other.

Myth: Low carb diets always lead to high cholesterol levels.

Fact: While it's true that some low carb diets may initially result in an increase in cholesterol levels, particularly in LDL cholesterol (often referred to as "bad" cholesterol), it's essential to distinguish between different types of cholesterol and understand the broader context of health outcomes. Research has shown that the quality of carbohydrates consumed, as well as other dietary and lifestyle factors, can significantly impact cholesterol levels. Furthermore, low carb diets often lead to improvements in other markers of cardiovascular health, such as triglyceride levels and HDL cholesterol (often referred to as "good" cholesterol), which are equally important in assessing overall heart health.

Myth: All cholesterol is harmful and should be avoided.

Fact: Cholesterol is a crucial substance necessary for various physiological functions in the body, including the production of hormones and the formation of cell membranes. While high levels of LDL cholesterol can increase the risk of cardiovascular disease, it's essential to recognize that cholesterol is not inherently harmful. Instead, it's the balance of different types of cholesterol and their interaction with other factors, such as inflammation and oxidative stress, that ultimately determines their impact on health. By focusing on overall dietary patterns and lifestyle habits, individuals can promote a healthier balance of cholesterol levels and reduce their risk of heart disease.

Myth: Low carb diets are restrictive and difficult to follow long-term.

Fact: While transitioning to a low carb diet may require some adjustments initially, many people find that they can adapt to this way of eating and sustain it over the long term with proper planning and support. Moreover, the increasing availability of low carb-friendly foods and resources makes it easier than ever to enjoy a varied and satisfying diet while reaping the health benefits associated with low carb eating. By focusing on whole, nutrient-dense foods and incorporating a diverse range of ingredients and flavors, individuals can create delicious and fulfilling meals that support their health goals while satisfying their taste buds.

In summary, understanding the relationship between low carb diets and cholesterol requires dispelling common myths and embracing evidence-based facts. By adopting a balanced approach to nutrition and lifestyle, individuals can harness the power of low carb eating to optimize their cholesterol levels and promote overall health and well-being.

Importance of Anti-Inflammatory Foods for Health

Inflammation is a natural response by the body's immune system to protect against harmful stimuli, such as pathogens, injury, or toxins. However, chronic inflammation, characterized by sustained activation of the immune system, has been linked to the development of various chronic diseases, including heart disease, diabetes, and certain types of cancer. Fortunately, the foods we eat can play a significant role in modulating inflammation levels and promoting overall health and well-being.

1. Reducing Chronic Disease Risk:

Anti-inflammatory foods are rich in nutrients, antioxidants, and bioactive compounds that help counteract inflammation and oxidative stress in the body. By incorporating a variety of these foods into your diet, you can help reduce your risk of developing chronic diseases associated with inflammation, such as cardiovascular disease, arthritis, and inflammatory bowel disease.

2. Supporting Immune Function:

A healthy immune system relies on a delicate balance between pro-inflammatory and anti-inflammatory signals. Consuming a diet rich in anti-inflammatory foods helps maintain this balance by providing the essential nutrients and compounds needed to regulate immune responses effectively. By supporting immune function, anti-inflammatory foods can help protect against infections and promote overall resilience and vitality.

3. Promoting Gut Health:

The gut microbiota, composed of trillions of microorganisms living in the digestive tract, plays a crucial role in regulating inflammation and immune function. Certain foods, such as fiber-rich fruits and vegetables, fermented foods, and omega-3 fatty acids, help nourish beneficial gut bacteria and promote a healthy balance of microbial diversity. By fostering a thriving gut microbiome, anti-inflammatory foods can enhance digestion, nutrient absorption, and overall gastrointestinal health.

4. Enhancing Brain Health:

Mounting evidence suggests a strong link between chronic inflammation and cognitive decline, neurodegenerative diseases, and mood disorders. Anti-inflammatory foods, particularly those rich in omega-3 fatty acids, polyphenols, and antioxidants, have been shown to support brain health and cognitive function by reducing inflammation, protecting against oxidative stress, and promoting neuroplasticity. Incorporating these foods into your diet may help preserve memory, concentration, and mood stability as you age.

5. Achieving Optimal Weight and Body Composition:

Inflammation is closely intertwined with metabolic health and obesity. Adipose tissue, or fat cells, produces pro-inflammatory molecules that contribute to systemic inflammation and insulin resistance. By adopting a diet focused on anti-inflammatory foods, you can help mitigate inflammation, improve insulin sensitivity, and support healthy weight management. Additionally, many anti-inflammatory foods are nutrient-dense and low in refined sugars and processed ingredients, making them ideal choices for promoting satiety and reducing cravings.

Navigating Your Low Carb Journey: Tips for Beginners

Embarking on a low carb journey can be both exciting and daunting, especially if you're new to this dietary approach. Whether you're seeking to improve your health, manage your weight, or simply explore new culinary horizons, these tips for beginners will help you navigate your low carb journey with confidence and success.

1. Educate Yourself: Take the time to learn about the principles behind low carb eating, including how it affects your body, potential benefits, and common misconceptions. Understanding the science and rationale behind the low carb approach will empower you to make informed decisions and stay motivated on your journey.

2. Start Slowly: Transitioning to a low carb diet overnight can be challenging and overwhelming. Instead, ease into it gradually by gradually reducing your intake of high-carb foods while increasing your consumption of low carb alternatives. This gradual approach will give your body time to adjust and minimize potential side effects like cravings and fatigue.

3. Focus on Whole Foods: Base your meals around whole, minimally processed foods that are naturally low in carbohydrates, such as vegetables, fruits, nuts, seeds, lean proteins, and healthy fats. These nutrient-dense foods not only provide essential vitamins, minerals, and antioxidants but also help stabilize blood sugar levels and promote satiety.

4. Pay Attention to Portion Sizes: While low carb eating can be satisfying, it's still essential to practice portion control and mindful eating. Be mindful of serving sizes and listen to your body's hunger and fullness cues to avoid overeating. Experiment with different meal compositions and portion sizes to find what works best for you.

5. Stay Hydrated: Adequate hydration is essential for overall health and well-being, especially when following a low carb diet. Drinking plenty of water helps flush out toxins, support digestion, and prevent dehydration, which can sometimes occur as your body adjusts to burning fat for fuel.

6. Plan and Prepare Ahead: Planning and preparation are key to success on a low carb diet. Take the time to plan your meals and snacks in advance, make a shopping list, and stock your kitchen with low carb essentials. Batch cooking and meal prepping can also save time and make it easier to stick to your dietary goals during busy days.

7. Be Flexible and Listen to Your Body: Remember that everyone's nutritional needs and preferences are unique. Don't be afraid to experiment with different foods, recipes, and meal timings to find what works best for you.

8. Seek Support and Accountability: Surround yourself with a supportive community of friends, family, or online forums who share your goals and can offer encouragement, advice, and motivation along the way. Having a support system can make all the difference in staying committed to your low carb journey, especially during challenging times.

By implementing these tips for beginners, you can embark on your low carb journey with confidence, resilience, and excitement. Remember that Rome wasn't built in a day, and progress is made one step at a time. Stay patient, stay consistent, and trust in the process as you work towards achieving your health and wellness goals.

Chapter 1: The Basics of Low Carb and Cholesterol

Understanding the fundamentals of low carb diets and their relationship with cholesterol is essential for anyone considering adopting this dietary approach. In this section, we'll explore the basic principles of low carb eating and how it impacts cholesterol levels in the body.

What Are Low Carb Diets?

Low carb diets, as the name suggests, are dietary patterns that restrict the intake of carbohydrates while emphasizing the consumption of protein, healthy fats, and non-starchy vegetables. By reducing carbohydrate intake, low carb diets aim to lower blood sugar levels, improve insulin sensitivity, and promote fat burning for energy.

How Low Carb Diets Impact Cholesterol Levels

Low carb diets have been shown to have various effects on cholesterol levels, which can vary depending on individual factors such as genetics, baseline cholesterol levels, and specific dietary choices. Some key points to consider include:

- Decrease in Triglycerides: One of the most significant benefits of low carb diets is their ability to lower triglyceride levels, a type of fat found in the bloodstream. By reducing carbohydrate intake, low carb diets can decrease triglyceride production in the liver, leading to improvements in cardiovascular health.

- Changes in LDL Cholesterol: Low carb diets may result in changes in LDL cholesterol (often referred to as "bad" cholesterol) levels, with some studies showing an increase in LDL cholesterol, particularly in individuals consuming high amounts of saturated fats. However, it's important to note that not all LDL cholesterol is created equal, and the size and density of LDL particles may be more relevant than total LDL cholesterol levels in assessing cardiovascular risk.

- Increase in HDL Cholesterol: Low carb diets have been associated with increases in HDL cholesterol (often referred to as "good" cholesterol), which plays a protective role in cardiovascular health by removing excess cholesterol from the bloodstream and transporting it to the liver for excretion.

Understanding Good and Bad Cholesterol

Cholesterol is a waxy substance found in the bloodstream and is essential for various physiological functions, including cell membrane structure, hormone production, and bile acid synthesis. Know that, not all cholesterol are/is created equal/same:

- LDL Cholesterol: Low-density lipoprotein (LDL) cholesterol is often referred to as "bad" cholesterol because high levels of LDL cholesterol are associated with an increased risk of cardiovascular disease. LDL cholesterol contributes to plaque buildup in the arteries, resulting to atherosclerosis aswell as increased risks of stroke and heart attack
- HDL Cholesterol: High-density lipoprotein (HDL) cholesterol is

often referred to as "good" cholesterol because high levels of HDL cholesterol are associated with a reduced risk of cardiovascular disease. HDL cholesterol helps remove excess cholesterol from the bloodstream and transports it to the liver for excretion, thus reducing the risk of plaque buildup in the arteries.

In summary, while low carb diets may impact cholesterol levels in different ways, they have been shown to offer numerous benefits for cardiovascular health, including reducing triglycerides and increasing HDL cholesterol. However, it's essential to consider the quality of dietary fats consumed on a low carb diet and to monitor cholesterol levels regularly, especially for individuals with pre-existing cardiovascular risk factors. Working with a healthcare professional or registered dietitian can help tailor a low carb eating plan that meets individual needs and promotes overall health and well-being.

DO YOU KNOW;Recent research has associated the Mediterranean diet with reduced heart disease risk indicators like elevated cholesterol and blood pressure. Presently, American nutrition specialists advocate for the Mediterranean diet as one of the beneficial dietary regimens.

CLICK HERE FOR YOUR FREE MEDITERRANEAN EBOOK!!

Chapter 2: Anti-Inflammatory Nutrition

In recent years, there has been growing recognition of the profound impact that inflammation has on overall health and well-being. Chronic inflammation is now understood to play a significant role in the development of various chronic diseases, including cardiovascular disease, diabetes, cancer, and neurodegenerative disorders. Fortunately, emerging research suggests that dietary choices can profoundly influence the body's inflammatory response, with certain foods possessing powerful anti-inflammatory properties. In this section, we'll delve extensively into anti-inflammatory nutrition, exploring the role of inflammation in health, identifying foods that trigger inflammation, and providing a comprehensive guide to incorporating anti-inflammatory foods into your diet.

The Role of Inflammation in Health

Inflammation is a natural and necessary response by the body's immune system to protect against injury, infection, and other threats to health. When tissues are damaged or exposed to harmful stimuli, the immune system initiates an inflammatory cascade, releasing various chemicals and immune cells to neutralize the threat and promote tissue repair. Acute inflammation is typically short-lived and resolves once the threat has been eliminated. However, chronic inflammation, characterized by persistent activation of the immune system, can have detrimental effects on health.

Chronic inflammation is now recognized as a key underlying factor in the pathogenesis of numerous chronic diseases. Prolonged exposure to inflammatory triggers, such as poor diet, sedentary lifestyle, stress, environmental toxins, and chronic infections, can disrupt the delicate balance of the immune system, leading to systemic inflammation. Over time, chronic inflammation can damage tissues, organs, and blood vessels, contributing to the development and progression of conditions such as atherosclerosis, insulin resistance, autoimmune diseases, and cancer.

Foods That Trigger Inflammation

The modern Western diet, characterized by excessive consumption of refined carbohydrates, processed foods, sugary beverages, unhealthy fats, and additives, has been implicated as a major contributor to chronic inflammation. Certain dietary components, such as refined sugars, trans fats, omega-6 fatty acids, artificial additives, and excessive salt, can trigger inflammatory responses in the body by promoting oxidative stress, disrupting gut microbiota balance, and activating pro-inflammatory signaling pathways.

Examples of foods that may promote inflammation include:

- Refined carbohydrates: White bread, pastries, sugary cereals, and other refined grains can cause spikes in blood sugar and insulin levels, leading to inflammation and insulin resistance.
- Trans fats: Found in fried foods, margarine, processed snacks, and commercially baked goods, trans fats are known to promote inflammation, impair endothelial function, and increase the risk of cardiovascular disease.
- Omega-6 fatty acids: Sources of omega-6 fatty acids include vegetable oils (soybean, corn,

sunflower, safflower), processed foods, and conventionally raised meats.

- Sugary beverages: Sweetened beverages such as soda, fruit juice, energy drinks, and sweetened teas are high in added sugars, which can contribute to inflammation, insulin resistance, and metabolic dysfunction.

Anti-Inflammatory Foods: Your Ultimate Guide

Fortunately, nature provides a wealth of foods rich in nutrients, antioxidants, and bioactive compounds that possess potent anti-inflammatory properties. By incorporating these foods into your diet regularly, you can help modulate inflammation, support immune function, and promote overall health and well-being. Here are some of the top anti-inflammatory foods to include in your diet:

- Fatty fish: Cold-water fatty fish such as salmon, mackerel, sardines, and trout are rich in omega-3 fatty acids, which have been shown to reduce inflammation, lower triglyceride levels, and support cardiovascular health.
- Leafy greens: Dark, leafy greens such as spinach, kale, Swiss chard, and collard greens are packed with vitamins, minerals, and phytochemicals that possess anti-

inflammatory properties. They also provide fiber, which supports gut health and regulates inflammation.

- Berries: Berries such as blueberries, strawberries, raspberries, and blackberries are loaded with antioxidants, including flavonoids and anthocyanins, which help combat oxidative stress and inflammation.
- Nuts and seeds: Almonds, walnuts, flaxseeds, chia seeds, and hemp seeds are excellent sources of healthy fats, fiber, and antioxidants that have been shown to reduce inflammation and improve cardiovascular health.
- Extra virgin olive oil: Extra virgin olive oil is rich in monounsaturated

fats and polyphenols, which have potent anti-inflammatory and antioxidant properties. Regular consumption of olive oil has been associated with a reduced risk of chronic diseases such as heart disease and cancer.

- Turmeric: Turmeric contains a compound called curcumin, which has powerful anti-inflammatory and antioxidant effects. Incorporating turmeric into your diet, either as a spice or as a supplement, may help reduce inflammation and alleviate symptoms of inflammatory conditions such as arthritis and inflammatory bowel disease.

In addition to these specific foods, adopting a whole foods-based diet that emphasizes fruits, vegetables, whole grains, legumes, and lean proteins can help reduce inflammation and support overall health. Minimizing or avoiding processed foods, refined sugars, unhealthy fats, and artificial additives is also essential for managing inflammation and promoting wellness.

In conclusion, anti-inflammatory nutrition is a powerful tool for combating chronic inflammation and promoting optimal health and well-being. By understanding the role of inflammation in health, identifying foods that trigger inflammation, and incorporating anti-inflammatory foods into your diet, you can help support your body's natural defense systems, reduce the risk of chronic diseases, and enhance your quality of life. Remember to focus on variety, balance, and moderation in your dietary choices, and consult with a healthcare professional or registered dietitian for personalized guidance and recommendations tailored to your individual needs and goals.

Chapter 3: Getting Started with Low Carb Cooking

Embarking on a low carb journey opens the door to a world of delicious, nutritious, and satisfying meals that support your health and well-being. In this chapter, we'll explore everything you need to know to get started with low carb cooking, from stocking your pantry with essential ingredients to mastering meal planning and prepping techniques. Whether you're a seasoned home cook or a novice in the kitchen, these tips and tricks will set you up for success on your low carb adventure.

Stocking Your Low Carb Pantry

Building a well-stocked pantry is the first step towards successful low carb cooking. By keeping a supply of essential ingredients on hand, you'll always be prepared to whip up delicious and nutritious meals without having to make last-minute trips to the grocery store. Here are some must-have items to include in your low carb pantry:

- **Healthy Fats:** Opt for high-quality sources of healthy fats such as extra virgin olive oil, coconut oil, avocado oil, and grass-fed butter or ghee. These fats are essential for flavor, satiety, and

nutrient absorption in low carb
cooking.

- **Proteins**: Stock up on a variety of
  protein sources, including lean
  meats (such as chicken, turkey,
  beef, and pork), fatty fish (such as
  salmon, mackerel, and sardines),
  eggs, tofu, tempeh, and (black
  beans, chickpeas, and lentils).

- **Low Carb Vegetables**: Load up
  on non-starchy vegetables such as
  leafy greens (spinach, kale,
  arugula), cruciferous vegetables
  (broccoli, cauliflower, Brussels
  sprouts), bell peppers, zucchini,
  mushrooms, and asparagus. These
  veggies are rich in fiber, vitamins,
  and minerals and are perfect for
  bulking up your meals.

- **Nuts and Seeds**: Keep a selection of nuts and seeds on hand for snacking or adding crunch and flavor to your dishes. Almonds, walnuts, pecans, pumpkin seeds, and sunflower seeds are all excellent choices.

- **Low Carb Flours and Sweeteners:** Experiment with alternative flours such as almond flour, coconut flour, and flaxseed meal for low carb baking and cooking. Stevia, erythritol, and monk fruit sweeteners are great options for adding sweetness without the carbs.

- **Herbs, Spices, and Seasonings:** Spice up your meals with a variety of herbs, spices, and seasonings to add depth and complexity of flavor. Essentials include garlic powder, onion powder, cumin, paprika, chili powder, dried herbs (such as oregano, thyme, basil), and sea salt.

- **Canned and Jarred Goods**: Keep your pantry stocked with canned goods such as diced tomatoes, tomato paste, coconut milk, broth, and canned fish (tuna, salmon).

Essential Kitchen Tools for Low Carb Cooking

Having the right kitchen tools and equipment can make low carb cooking a breeze and help you prepare delicious meals with ease and efficiency. Here are some essential kitchen tools to consider adding to your arsenal:

- High-Quality Knives: Invest in a set of sharp, high-quality knives for slicing, dicing, and chopping vegetables, meats, and other ingredients.

- Cutting Boards: Opt for cutting boards made of durable materials such as bamboo or plastic.
- Cookware: Invest in a variety of cookware, including pots, pans, skillets, and baking sheets, to accommodate different cooking methods such as sautéing, roasting, and baking.
- Food Processor or Blender: A food processor or blender is invaluable for making sauces, dressings, dips, and smoothies, as well as for chopping, pureeing, and blending ingredients.
- Vegetable Spiralizer: A vegetable spiralizer allows you to create low carb alternatives to pasta and noodles using vegetables such as

zucchini, carrots, and sweet potatoes.

- Slow Cooker or Instant Pot: These versatile appliances are perfect for cooking low carb soups, stews, and roasts with minimal effort and hands-on time.
- Measuring Cups and Spoons: Accurate measuring is essential for low carb cooking, especially when working with ingredients like flour, sweeteners, and spices. Invest in a set of measuring cups and spoons for precise portioning.
- Baking Essentials: If you plan to do low carb baking, make sure you have baking pans, mixing bowls, spatulas, whisks, and other baking essentials on hand.

Meal Planning and Prepping Tips

Meal planning and prepping are key strategies for staying on track with your low carb diet and avoiding the temptation of unhealthy convenience foods. Here are some tips for meal planning and preparation:

- Set Aside Time: Dedicate a specific day or time each week to plan your meals, make a grocery list, and prep ingredients. Consistency is key to success.
- Plan Balanced Meals: Aim to include a balance of protein, healthy fats, non-starchy vegetables, and low carb grains or

legumes in each meal to ensure you're getting a variety of nutrients and staying satisfied.

- Batch Cooking: Cook large batches of low carb staples such as grilled chicken, roasted vegetables, and quinoa or cauliflower rice to use as the building blocks for multiple meals throughout the week.
- Use Portion-Controlled Containers: Invest in portion-controlled containers or meal prep containers to portion out meals and snacks ahead of time for easy grab-and-go convenience.
- Label and Date: Label your meal prep containers with the contents and date of preparation to keep

track of freshness and avoid food waste.

- Mix and Match: Get creative with your meal prep by mixing and matching ingredients to create a variety of meals and flavors throughout the week. For example, use leftover roasted vegetables in salads, omelets, or grain bowls.

By stocking your pantry with essential ingredients, investing in quality kitchen tools and equipment, and implementing effective meal planning and prepping strategies, you'll be well-equipped to tackle low carb cooking with confidence and ease. With a little preparation and organization, you'll soon discover that low carb eating can be delicious, satisfying, and sustainable for long-term health and wellness.

Chapter 4: Breakfast Delights

In this chapter, we'll explore the refreshing world of low carb smoothies and juices, perfect for starting your day on a nutritious note. These recipes are not only delicious but also packed with vitamins, minerals, and antioxidants to fuel your body and keep you energized throughout the morning. Each recipe is simple to prepare and can be customized to suit your taste preferences and dietary needs.

Low Carb Smoothies and Juices

Low Carb Smoothies

1. Berry Blast Smoothie

Ingredients:

- 1/2 cup mixed berries (such as strawberries, blueberries, raspberries)
- 1/2 a cup of unsweetened almond milk (or any preferd milk of choice)
- 1/4 cup plain Greek yogurt
- 1 tablespoon almond butter or peanut butter

- 1 teaspoon chia seeds or ground flaxseeds (optional)
- Ice cubes (optional)

Preparation Time: 5 minutes

Method:

1. Combine the mixed berries, almond milk, Greek yogurt, almond butter or peanut butter, and chia seeds or ground flaxseeds (if using) in a blender.
2. Blend until smooth and creamy, adding ice cubes as desired for a thicker consistency.
3. Pour into a glass and serve.

2. Green Goddess Smoothie

Ingredients:

- 1 cup spinach leaves
- 1/2 ripe avocado, peeled and pitted
- 1/2 cup cucumber slices
- 1/2 cup unsweetened coconut water or almond milk
- Juice of 1/2 lime
- Fresh mint leaves for garnish (optional)

Preparation Time: 5 minutes

Method:

1. Place the spinach leaves, avocado, cucumber slices, coconut water or almond milk, and lime juice in a blender.
2. Blend until smooth and creamy, adding more liquid as needed to reach your desired consistency.
3. Pour the smoothie into a glass, garnish with fresh mint leaves if desired, and serve immediately.

3. Tropical Paradise Smoothie

Ingredients:

- 1/2 cup frozen pineapple chunks
- 1/2 cup frozen mango chunks
- 1/2 ripe banana (optional, omit for lower carb)

- 1/2 cup unsweetened almond or coconut milk
- 1 tablespoon unsweetened shredded coconut
- Splash of vanilla extract

Preparation Time: 5 minutes

Method:

1. Combine the frozen pineapple chunks, frozen mango chunks, banana (if using), coconut milk or almond milk, shredded coconut, and vanilla extract in a blender.
2. Blend until smooth and creamy, adjusting the consistency with additional liquid if necessary.

3. Pour the smoothie into a glass and serve immediately, optionally garnished with a sprinkle of shredded coconut on top.

4. Chocolate Peanut Butter Protein Smoothie

Ingredients:

- 1 scoop chocolate protein powder
- 1 tablespoon unsweetened cocoa powder
- 1 tablespoon natural peanut butter
- 1/2 ripe banana (optional, omit for lower carb)
- One(1) cup of unsweetened almond or coconut milk
- Ice cubes (optional)

Preparation Time: 5 minutes

Method:

1. Place the chocolate protein powder, cocoa powder, peanut butter, banana (if using), and almond milk or coconut milk in a blender.
2. Blend until smooth and creamy, adding ice cubes as desired for a thicker consistency.
3. Immediately,pour the smoothie into a glass and serve.

5. Keto Berry Avocado Smoothie

Ingredients:

- 1/2 ripe avocado, peeled and pitted
- 1/2 cup mixed berries (such as strawberries, blueberries, raspberries)
- 1/2 a cup unsweetened almond/coconut milk
- 1 tablespoon chia seeds or ground flaxseeds
- 1 tablespoon sugar-free sweetener (such as erythritol or monk fruit)
- Ice cubes (optional)

Preparation Time: 5 minutes

Method:

1. Combine the ripe avocado, mixed berries, almond milk or coconut milk, chia seeds or ground flaxseeds, and sugar-free sweetener in a blender.
2. Blend until smooth and creamy, adding ice cubes if desired for a colder, thicker smoothie.
3. Pour the smoothie into a glass.

Low Carb Juices

1. Green Detox Juice

Ingredients:

- 1 cucumber
- 2 stalks celery
- 1 handful spinach leaves
- 1/2 lemon, peeled

- 1 inch piece of ginger
- Ice cubes (optional)

Preparation Time: 5 minutes

Method:

1. Wash and chop the cucumber, celery, and ginger into smaller pieces.
2. Place the chopped vegetables and spinach leaves in a juicer, followed by the peeled lemon.
3. Juice the ingredients until very smooth and well combined.
4. Serve the juice over ice cubes for a refreshing drink.

2. Citrus Immunity Booster Juice

Ingredients:

- 2 oranges, peeled and segmented
- 1/2 grapefruit, peeled and segmented
- 1 inch piece of turmeric
- 1 inch piece of ginger
- Pinch of cayenne pepper (optional)
- Ice cubes (optional)

Preparation Time: 5 minutes

Method:

1. Juice the oranges and grapefruit segments in a juicer.

2. Add the turmeric, ginger, and cayenne pepper (if using) to the juicer.
3. Juice all the ingredients until very well combined and very smooth.
4. Serve the juice over ice cubes for an extra refreshing kick.

3. Beetroot Berry Blast Juice

Ingredients:

- 1 small beetroot, peeled and chopped
- 1/2 cup mixed berries (such as strawberries, raspberries, blueberries)
- 1 carrot, peeled and chopped
- 1/2 apple, cored and chopped

- 1 inch piece of ginger
- Ice cubes (optional)

Preparation Time: 5 minutes

Method:

1. Juice the beetroot, mixed berries, carrot, apple, and ginger in a juicer.
2. Continue juicing until all the ingredients are well combined and smooth.
3. Serve the juice over ice cubes for a cool and refreshing drink.

4. Cucumber Mint Cooler Juice

Ingredients:

- 2 cucumbers
- 1/2 cup fresh mint leaves
- 1/2 lime, peeled
- 1 teaspoon honey or sugar-free sweetener (optional)
- Ice cubes (optional)

Preparation Time: 5 minutes

Method:

1. Wash and chop the cucumbers into smaller pieces.
2. Place the chopped cucumbers and fresh mint leaves in a juicer.
3. Juice the ingredients until smooth and well combined.

4. Add the peeled lime to the juicer and continue juicing until fully incorporated.

5. Sweeten the juice with honey or sugar-free sweetener if desired.

6. Serve the juice over ice cubes for a refreshing and hydrating drink.

5. Spicy Tomato Vegetable Juice

Ingredients:

- 2 large tomatoes
- 1 red bell pepper, seeds removed
- 2 stalks celery
- 1/2 cucumber
- 1/2 lemon, peeled
- Pinch of cayenne pepper
- Pinch of sea salt

- Ice cubes (optional)

Preparation Time: 5 minutes

Method:

1. Wash and chop the tomatoes, red bell pepper, celery, and cucumber into smaller pieces.
2. Place the chopped vegetables in a juicer.
3. Juice the ingredients until.
4. Add the peeled lemon, cayenne pepper, and sea salt to the juicer.
5. Continue juicing until all the ingredients are fully incorporated.
6. Serve the juice over ice cubes for a zesty and invigorating drink.

These low carb smoothies and juices are perfect for incorporating into your breakfast routine or enjoying as a refreshing pick-me-up any time of day. With a variety of flavors and ingredients to choose from, you're sure to find a favorite that satisfies your taste buds and nourishes your body. Experiment with different combinations and ingredients to create your own custom blends and discover the perfect balance of flavor and nutrition. Cheers to a healthier, more vibrant you!

Egg-citing Breakfast Ideas

In this section, we'll explore a collection of egg-citing low carb pancake and waffle recipes that will kick-start your morning with flavor and energy. Whether you prefer the light and fluffy texture of pancakes or the crispy goodness of waffles, these recipes are sure to satisfy your breakfast cravings while keeping your carb intake in check. Each recipe is simple to prepare and can be customized with your favorite toppings and add-ins.

Energizing Low Carb Pancakes and Waffles

Low Carb Pancakes

1. Fluffy Coconut Flour Pancakes

Ingredients:

- 1/4 cup coconut flour
- 2 large eggs
- 1/4 cup unsweetened almond milk (or any milk of choice)
- 2 tablespoons coconut oil, melted
- 1 tablespoon sugar-free sweetener (such as erythritol or monk fruit)
- 1/2 teaspoon baking powder
- 1/2 teaspoon vanilla extract
- Pinch of salt
- Optional toppings: sugar-free maple syrup, fresh berries, whipped cream

Preparation Time: 15 minutes

Method:

1. In a bowl, whisk together the coconut flour, sugar-free sweetener, baking powder, and salt.
2. In a separate bowl, beat the eggs until covered with a mass of small bubbles. Stir in the almond milk, melted coconut oil, and vanilla extract.
3. Gradually add the dry ingredients to the wet ingredients, stirring until well combined and smooth.
4. Heat a non-stick skillet or griddle over medium heat and lightly grease with coconut oil or cooking spray.
5. Pour 2-3 tablespoons of batter onto the skillet for each pancake,

spreading it out slightly with the back of a spoon.

6. Cook for 2-3 minutes, or until bubbles form on the surface of the pancake and the edges begin to set.

7. Flip over them pancakes and cook for additional 1-3 minutes, preferably until golden brown and cooked all through.

8. Repeat with the remaining batter.

9. Serve hot with your favorite toppings.

2. Almond Flour Pancakes with Blueberries

Ingredients:

- 1 cup almond flour
- 2 large eggs
- 1/4 cup unsweetened almond milk (or any milk of choice)
- 1 tablespoon coconut oil, melted
- 1 tablespoon sugar-free sweetener (such as erythritol or monk fruit)
- 1/2 teaspoon baking powder
- 1/2 teaspoon vanilla extract
- Pinch of salt
- 1/2 cup fresh blueberries
- Optional toppings: sugar-free maple syrup, additional blueberries, sliced almonds

Preparation Time: 15 minutes

Method:

1. In a bowl, whisk together the almond flour, sugar-free sweetener, baking powder, and salt.
2. In a separate bowl, beat the eggs until covered with a mass of small bubbles. Stir in the almond milk, melted coconut oil, and vanilla extract.
3. Gradually add the dry ingredients to the wet ingredients, stirring until well combined and smooth.
4. Gently fold in the fresh blueberries.
5. Heat a non-stick skillet or griddle over medium heat and lightly grease with coconut oil or cooking spray.

6. Pour 2-3 tablespoons of batter onto the skillet for each pancake, spreading it out slightly with the back of a spoon.
7. Cook for 2-3 minutes, or until bubbles form on the surface of the pancake and the edges begin to set.
8. Flip over them pancakes and cook for additional 1-3 minutes, preferably until golden brown and cooked all through.
9. Repeat with the remaining batter.
10. Serve hot with your favorite toppings.

3. Keto Cream Cheese Pancakes

Ingredients:

- 2 oz cream cheese, softened
- 2 large eggs
- 1 tablespoon coconut flour (optional, for thicker pancakes)
- 1 tablespoon sugar-free sweetener (such as erythritol or monk fruit)
- 1/2 teaspoon vanilla extract
- Pinch of cinnamon (optional)
- Butter or coconut oil for cooking
- Optional toppings: sugar-free maple syrup, sliced strawberries, whipped cream

Preparation Time: 10 minutes

Method:

1. In a bowl, beat the softened cream cheese until smooth.

2. Add the eggs, coconut flour (if using), sugar-free sweetener, vanilla extract, and cinnamon (if using) to the bowl.

3. Mix until well combined and smooth.

4. Heat a non-stick skillet or griddle over medium heat and lightly grease with butter or coconut oil.

5. Pour about 2 tablespoons of batter onto the skillet for each pancake, spreading it out slightly with the back of a spoon.

6. Cook for 2-3 minutes, or until bubbles form on the surface of the pancake and the edges begin to set.

7. Flip over them pancakes and cook for additional 1-3 minutes,

preferably until golden brown and cooked all through.

8. Repeat with the remaining batter.
9. Serve hot with your favorite toppings.

4. Pumpkin Spice Pancakes

Ingredients:

- 1/4 cup pumpkin puree
- 2 large eggs
- 2 tablespoons almond flour
- 1 tablespoon coconut flour
- 1 tablespoon sugar-free sweetener (such as erythritol or monk fruit)
- 1/2 teaspoon baking powder
- 1/2 teaspoon pumpkin pie spice
- Pinch of salt

- Butter or coconut oil for cooking
- Optional toppings: sugar-free maple syrup, chopped pecans, whipped cream

Preparation Time: 15 minutes

Method:

1. In a bowl, whisk together the pumpkin puree, eggs, almond flour, coconut flour, sugar-free sweetener, baking powder, pumpkin pie spice, and salt until well combined.
2. Heat a non-stick skillet or griddle over medium heat and lightly grease with butter or coconut oil.

3. Pour about 2 tablespoons of batter onto the skillet for each pancake, spreading it out slightly with the back of a spoon.
4. Cook for 2-3 minutes, or until bubbles form on the surface of the pancake and the edges begin to set.
5. Flip the pancakes and cook for an additional 1-2 minutes, or until golden brown and cooked through.
6. Repeat with the remaining batter, greasing the skillet as needed.
7. Serve the pancakes hot with your favorite toppings.

5. Lemon Ricotta Pancakes

Ingredients:

- 1 cup ricotta cheese
- 2 large eggs
- 1 tablespoon lemon zest
- 1 tablespoon lemon juice
- 2 tablespoons almond flour
- 1 tablespoon sugar-free sweetener (such as erythritol or monk fruit)
- 1/2 teaspoon baking powder
- Pinch of salt
- Butter or coconut oil for cooking
- Optional toppings: sugar-free maple syrup, fresh berries, whipped cream

Preparation Time: 15 minutes

Method:

1. In a bowl, whisk together the ricotta cheese, eggs, lemon zest, and lemon juice until smooth.
2. Add the almond flour, sugar-free sweetener, baking powder, and salt to the bowl, and mix until well combined.
3. Heat a non-stick skillet or griddle over medium heat and lightly grease with butter or coconut oil.
4. Pour about 2 tablespoons of batter onto the skillet for each pancake, spreading it out slightly with the back of a spoon.
5. Cook for 2-3 minutes, or until bubbles form on the surface of the pancake and the edges begin to set.

6. Flip over them pancakes and cook for additional 1-3 minutes, preferably until golden brown and cooked all through.
7. Repeat with the remaining batter.
8. Serve hot with your favorite toppings.

Low Carb Waffles

1. Classic Almond Flour Waffles

Ingredients:

- 1 cup almond flour
- 2 large eggs
- 1/4 cup unsweetened almond milk (or any milk of choice)
- 2 tablespoons coconut oil, melted

- 1 tablespoon sugar-free sweetener (such as erythritol or monk fruit)
- 1/2 teaspoon baking powder
- 1/2 teaspoon vanilla extract
- Pinch of salt
- Optional toppings: sugar-free maple syrup, fresh berries, whipped cream

Preparation Time: 15 minutes

Method:

1. In a bowl, whisk together the almond flour, sugar-free sweetener, baking powder, and salt.
2. In a different bowl/plate, whisk the eggs until frothy. Stir in the

almond milk, melted coconut oil, and vanilla extract.

3. Gradually add the dry ingredients to the wet ingredients, stirring until well combined and smooth.

4. Preheat the waffle iron according to the manufacturing instructions.

5. Lightly grease the waffle iron with coconut oil or cooking spray.

6. Pour the batter onto the waffle iron, making sure to spread it out evenly.

7. Close the waffle iron and cook according to manufacturer's instructions, or until the waffles are golden brown and crispy.

8. Remove the waffles from the iron and serve with toppings.

2. Coconut Flour Waffles

Ingredients:

- 1/2 cup coconut flour
- 4 large eggs
- 1/4 cup unsweetened almond milk (or any milk of choice)
- 2 tablespoons coconut oil, melted
- 1 tablespoon sugar-free sweetener (such as erythritol or monk fruit)
- 1/2 teaspoon baking powder
- 1/2 teaspoon vanilla extract
- Pinch of salt
- Optional toppings: sugar-free maple syrup, fresh berries, whipped cream

Preparation Time: 15 minutes

Method:

1. In a bowl, whisk together the coconut flour, sugar-free sweetener, baking powder, and salt.
2. In a separate bowl, beat the eggs until frothy. Stir in the almond milk, melted coconut oil, and vanilla extract.
3. Gradually add the dry ingredients to the wet ingredients, stirring until well combined and smooth.
4. Preheat your waffle iron according to manufacturer's instructions.
5. Lightly grease the waffle iron with coconut oil or cooking spray.

6. Pour the batter onto the preheated waffle iron, spreading it out evenly.

7. Close the waffle iron and cook according to manufacturer's instructions, or until the waffles are golden brown and crispy.

8. Carefully remove the waffles from the iron and serve immediately with your favorite toppings.

3. Keto Chaffle Waffles

Ingredients:

- 1/2 cup shredded mozzarella cheese
- 1 large egg

- Optional add-ins: 1 tablespoon almond flour, 1/2 teaspoon baking powder, 1/2 teaspoon vanilla extract, sugar-free sweetener to taste
- Optional toppings: sugar-free maple syrup, fresh berries, whipped cream

Preparation Time: 10 minutes

Method:

1. Preheat your mini waffle maker according to manufacturer's instructions.
2. In a bowl, whisk the egg until well beaten.

3. Stir in the shredded mozzarella cheese and any optional add-ins you desire until combined.
4. Spoon half of the mixture onto the preheated waffle maker, close the lid, and cook for 3-4 minutes or until golden and crispy.
5. Repeat with the remaining mixture.
6. Serve the chaffle waffles hot with your favorite toppings.

4. Pumpkin Spice Waffles

Ingredients:

- 1/2 cup almond flour
- 2 large eggs
- 1/4 cup pumpkin puree

- 2 tablespoons coconut oil, melted
- 1 tablespoon sugar-free sweetener (such as erythritol or monk fruit)
- 1/2 teaspoon baking powder
- 1/2 teaspoon pumpkin pie spice
- Pinch of salt
- Optional toppings: sugar-free maple syrup, chopped pecans, whipped cream

Preparation Time: 15 minutes

Method:

1. In a bowl, whisk together the almond flour, sugar-free sweetener, baking powder, pumpkin pie spice, and salt.

2. In a separate bowl, beat the eggs until frothy. Stir in the pumpkin puree, melted coconut oil, and vanilla extract.

3. Gradually add the dry ingredients to the wet ingredients, stirring until well combined and smooth.

4. Preheat your waffle iron according to manufacturer's instructions.

5. Lightly grease the waffle iron with coconut oil or cooking spray.

6. Pour the batter onto the preheated waffle iron, spreading it out evenly.

7. Close the waffle iron and cook according to manufacturer's instructions, or until the waffles are golden brown and crispy.

8. Carefully remove the waffles from the iron and serve immediately with your favorite toppings.

5. Lemon Poppy Seed Waffles

Ingredients:

- 1 cup almond flour
- 2 large eggs
- 1/4 cup unsweetened almond milk (or any milk of choice)
- 2 tablespoons coconut oil, melted
- 1 tablespoon sugar-free sweetener (such as erythritol or monk fruit)
- 1 tablespoon lemon zest
- 1 tablespoon lemon juice
- 1 tablespoon poppy seeds
- 1/2 teaspoon baking powder

- Pinch of salt
- Optional toppings: sugar-free maple syrup, fresh berries, whipped cream

Preparation Time: 15 minutes

Method:

1. In a bowl, whisk together the almond flour, sugar-free sweetener, baking powder, lemon zest, lemon juice, poppy seeds, and salt.
2. In a bowl, beat the eggs till frothy. Stir in the almond milk, melted coconut oil, and vanilla extract.

3. Gradually add the dry ingredients to the wet ingredients, stirring until well combined and smooth.
4. Preheat your waffle iron.
5. Lightly grease the waffle iron with coconut oil or cooking spray.
6. Pour the batter onto the preheated waffle iron.
7. Close the waffle iron and cook according to manufacturer's instructions, or until the waffles are golden brown and crispy.
8. Remove the waffles from the iron and serve with your favorite toppings.

Chapter 5: Satisfying Soups and Salads

In this chapter, we'll delve into the world of satisfying soups and refreshing salads, perfect for those seeking low-carb options without sacrificing flavor or nutrition. Whether you're looking for a comforting bowl of creamy soups or a vibrant salad bursting with fresh ingredients, these recipes are sure to delight your taste buds and keep you feeling satisfied.

Creamy Low Carb Soups

Creamy soups are a comforting and satisfying option, especially during colder months. Here are five simple recipes for creamy low-carb soups:

1. Creamy Broccoli Soup

Ingredients:

- 2 cups broccoli florets
- 1 small onion, diced
- 2 cloves garlic, minced
- 2 cups vegetable or chicken broth
- 1/2 cup heavy cream
- 2 tablespoons butter
- Salt and pepper to taste

Preparation Time: 30 minutes

Method:

1. In a pot,over medium heat, melt the butter. Add the diced onion and minced garlic, cook until soft.
2. Add the broccoli florets to the pot and sauté for a few minutes.
3. Pour in the broth and allow simmer. Cook until the broccoli is tender, about 15 minutes.
4. Use a blender to puree the soup until very smooth. Or preferably,transfer the soup to a blender and blend.
5. Stir in the heavy cream and add salt and pepper to taste.
6. Allow to cook for an additional 5 minutes, then serve hot.

2. Creamy Cauliflower Soup

Ingredients:

- 1 head cauliflower, chopped
- 1 small onion, diced
- 2 cloves garlic, minced
- 2 cups vegetable or chicken broth
- 1/2 cup heavy cream
- 2 tablespoons butter
- Salt and pepper to taste

Preparation Time: 30 minutes

Method:

1. In large pot, melt the butter . Add the diced onion and minced garlic, and cook until soft.

2. Add the chopped cauliflower to the pot and sauté for a few minutes.
3. Pour in the broth and allow to simmer. Cook until the cauliflower is tender, about 15 minutes.
4. Using an immersion blender, puree the soup until smooth. Add in the heavy cream and season with salt and pepper to taste.
5. Allow to cook for an additional 5 minutes, then serve hot.

3. Creamy Mushroom Soup

Ingredients:

- 8 oz mushrooms, sliced
- 1 small onion, diced
- 2 cloves garlic, minced
- 2 cups vegetable or chicken broth
- 1/2 cup heavy cream
- 2 tablespoons butter
- Salt and pepper to taste

Preparation Time: 30 minutes

Method:

1. In a large pot, melt the butter over medium heat. Add the diced onion and minced garlic, and cook until softened.
2. Add the sliced mushrooms to the pot and sauté until they release their juices.

3. Pour in the broth and bring to a simmer. Cook for about 15 minutes.
4. Use an immersion blender to puree the soup until smooth. Alternatively, transfer the soup to a blender and blend until smooth.
5. Stir in the heavy cream and season with salt and pepper to taste.
6. Cook for an additional 5 minutes, then serve hot.

4. Creamy Spinach Soup

Ingredients:

- 4 cups fresh spinach leaves
- 1 small onion, diced
- 2 cloves garlic, minced
- 2 cups vegetable or chicken broth
- 1/2 cup heavy cream
- 2 tablespoons butter
- Salt and pepper to taste

Preparation Time: 30 minutes

Method:

1. In a big pot, melt the butter. Add the diced onion and minced garlic, and cook until softened.
2. Add the fresh spinach leaves to the pot and sauté until wilted.
3. Pour in the broth, allow simmer. Cook for about 15 minutes.

4. Transfer the soup to a blender and blend until smooth.
5. Stir in the heavy cream and season with salt and pepper to taste.
6. Cook for an additional 5 minutes, then serve hot.

5. Creamy Tomato Soup

Ingredients:

- 1 can (14 oz) diced tomatoes
- 1 small onion, diced
- 2 cloves garlic, minced
- 2 cups vegetable or chicken broth
- 1/2 cup heavy cream

- 2 tablespoons butter
- Salt and pepper to taste

Preparation Time: 30 minutes

Method:

1. In a pot, melt the butter over low heat. Add the onion and minced garlic, and cook.
2. Add the diced tomatoes to the pot and cook for a few minutes.
3. Pour in the broth and bring to a simmer. Cook for about 15 minutes.
4. Transfer the soup to a blender and blend until smooth.
5. Stir in the heavy cream and season with salt and pepper to taste.

6. Cook for an additional 5 minutes, then serve hot.

Refreshing Salad Combinations

Salads are versatile and refreshing, making them perfect for any meal or occasion. Here are five simple recipes for refreshing salad combinations:

1. Classic Caesar Salad

Ingredients:

- 1 head romaine lettuce, chopped
- 1/4 cup grated Parmesan cheese
- 1/4 cup Caesar dressing

- Salt and pepper to taste
- Croutons (optional)

Preparation Time: 10 minutes

Method:

1. In a large bowl, combine the chopped romaine lettuce and grated Parmesan cheese.
2. Add Caesar dressing to taste and toss until evenly coated.
3. Season with salt and pepper, and add croutons if desired.
4. Serve immediately as a side or add grilled chicken for a complete meal.

2. Greek Salad

Ingredients:

- 2 large tomatoes, chopped
- 1 cucumber, sliced
- 1/2 red onion, thinly sliced
- 1/2 cup Kalamata olives
- 1/2 cup crumbled feta cheese
- 2 tablespoons extra virgin olive oil
- 1 tablespoon red wine vinegar
- 1 teaspoon dried oregano
- Salt and pepper to taste

Preparation Time: 15 minutes

Method:

1. In a large bowl, combine the chopped tomatoes, sliced cucumber, sliced red onion,

Kalamata olives, and crumbled feta cheese.

2. In a bowl, whisk the olive oil, red wine vinegar, dried oregano, salt, and pepper together to make the dressing.

3. Drizzle the dressing over the salad and combine.

4. Serve immediately as a refreshing side dish or light lunch.

3. Caprese Salad

Ingredients:

- 2 large tomatoes, sliced
- 1 ball fresh mozzarella cheese, sliced
- Fresh basil leaves

- 2 tablespoons extra virgin olive oil
- 1 tablespoon balsamic glaze (optional)
- Salt and pepper to taste

Preparation Time: 10 minutes

Method:

1. By alternating them, arrange the tomato slices and mozzarella slices on a serving platter.
2. Tuck fresh basil leaves in between the tomato and mozzarella slices.
3. Drizzle extra virgin olive oil over the salad.
4. If using, drizzle balsamic glaze over the salad in a zigzag pattern.

5. Season with salt and pepper to taste.
6. Serve immediately as a refreshing appetizer or side dish.

4. Avocado and Spinach Salad

Ingredients:

- 2 cups fresh spinach leaves
- 1 ripe avocado, diced
- 1/4 cup cherry tomatoes, halved
- 1/4 cup sliced almonds
- 2 tablespoons feta cheese, crumbled
- 2 tablespoons extra virgin olive oil
- 1 tablespoon lemon juice
- Salt and pepper to taste

Preparation Time: 10 minutes

Method:

1. In a large bowl, combine the fresh spinach leaves, diced avocado, cherry tomatoes, sliced almonds, and crumbled feta cheese.
2. In a small bowl, whisk together the extra virgin olive oil, lemon juice, salt, and pepper to make the dressing.
3. Drizzle the dressing over the salad and toss.
4. Serve immediately as a nutritious side dish or add grilled chicken for a complete meal.

5. Cobb Salad

Ingredients:

- 2 cups mixed salad greens
- 1/2 cup cooked chicken breast, diced
- 2 hard-boiled eggs, sliced
- 1 avocado, diced
- 1/4 cup crumbled blue cheese
- 1/4 cup diced tomatoes
- 2 slices cooked bacon, crumbled
- 2 tablespoons ranch dressing

Preparation Time: 15 minutes

Method:

1. Arrange the mixed salad greens on a serving platter.

2. Arrange the diced chicken breast, sliced hard-boiled eggs, diced avocado, crumbled blue cheese, diced tomatoes, and crumbled bacon in rows on top of the salad greens.
3. Drizzle ranch dressing over the salad or serve it on the side.
4. Serve immediately as a hearty and satisfying meal option.

These creamy soups and refreshing salads are not only low in carbs but also bursting with flavour and nutrients. Whether you're looking for a comforting meal or a light and refreshing dish, these recipes are sure to satisfy your cravings and keep you feeling energized throughout the day.

Hearty and Filling Soup-Salad Combos

Combining a hearty soup with a refreshing salad creates a balanced and satisfying meal. These soup-salad combos offer a mix of flavors, textures, and nutrients to keep you feeling full and nourished. Here are three delicious and filling recipes:

1. Minestrone Soup with Mixed Greens Salad

Minestrone Soup Ingredients:

- 2 tablespoons olive oil
- 1 onion, diced

- 2 carrots, diced
- 2 celery stalks, diced
- 3 cloves garlic, minced
- 1 can (14 oz) diced tomatoes
- 6 cups vegetable broth
- One cup small pasta ;such as ditalini or small shells
- (15 oz (one can,) kidney beans, well drained and rinsed
- 2 cups chopped spinach or kale
- 1 teaspoon dried oregano
- 1 teaspoon dried basil
- Salt and pepper to taste
- Grated Parmesan cheese for serving (optional)

Mixed Greens Salad Ingredients:

- 4 cups mixed salad greens

- 1/4 cup cherry tomatoes, halved
- 1/4 cup sliced cucumber
- 1/4 cup sliced red onion
- 2 tablespoons balsamic vinaigrette dressing

Preparation Time: 45 minutes

Method:

1. In a pot, heat up the olive oil. Add diced onion, carrots, and celery. Cook until softened, about 5 minutes.
2. Add minced garlic and cook for an additional 2 minutes.
3. Pour in diced tomatoes and vegetable broth. Bring to a boil,

then reduce heat and simmer for 20 minutes.

4. Add pasta, kidney beans, chopped spinach or kale, dried oregano, and dried basil to the pot. Cook for another 10 minutes, or until pasta is tender.

5. Season with salt and pepper to taste.

6. While the soup is simmering, prepare the mixed greens salad by combining salad greens, cherry tomatoes, sliced cucumber, and sliced red onion in a large bowl.

7. Drizzle balsamic vinaigrette dressing over the salad and toss until well coated.

8. Serve the minestrone soup hot, garnished with grated Parmesan

cheese if desired, alongside the mixed greens salad.

2. Chicken and Vegetable Soup with Greek Salad

Chicken and Vegetable Soup
Ingredients:

- 2 tablespoons olive oil
- 1 onion, diced
- 2 carrots, diced
- 2 celery stalks, diced
- 3 cloves garlic, minced
- 6 cups chicken broth
- 2 cups cooked shredded chicken
- 1 cup chopped zucchini
- 1 cup chopped green beans
- 1 cup diced potatoes

- 1 teaspoon dried thyme
- Salt and pepper to taste

Greek Salad Ingredients:

- 2 large tomatoes, chopped
- 1 cucumber, diced
- 1/2 red onion, thinly sliced
- 1/2 cup Kalamata olives
- 1/2 cup crumbled feta cheese
- 2 tablespoons extra virgin olive oil
- 1 tablespoon red wine vinegar
- 1 teaspoon dried oregano
- Salt and pepper to taste

Preparation Time: 45 minutes

Method:

1. In a large pot, heat olive oil over medium heat. Add diced onion, carrots, and celery. Cook until softened, about 5 minutes.
2. Add minced garlic and cook for an additional 2 minute.
3. Pour in chicken broth and bring to a boil. Add chopped zucchini, green beans, diced potatoes, and dried thyme. Simmer for 20 minutes, or until vegetables are tender.
4. Add cooked shredded chicken to the pot and cook for another 5 minutes.
5. Season with salt and pepper to taste.
6. While the soup is simmering, prepare the Greek salad by

combining chopped tomatoes, diced cucumber, thinly sliced red onion, Kalamata olives, and crumbled feta cheese in a large bowl.

7. In a small bowl, whisk together extra virgin olive oil, red wine vinegar, dried oregano, salt, and pepper to make the dressing.

8. Drizzle the dressing over the salad and toss until well combined.

9. Serve the chicken and vegetable soup hot, accompanied by the Greek salad.

3. Beef and Barley Soup with Spinach and Strawberry Salad

Beef and Barley Soup Ingredients:

- 2 tablespoons olive oil
- 1 lb beef stew meat, cut into small cubes
- 1 onion, diced
- 2 carrots, diced
- 2 celery stalks, diced
- 3 cloves garlic, minced
- 6 cups beef broth
- 1/2 cup pearl barley
- 1 cup diced tomatoes
- 2 cups chopped spinach
- 1 teaspoon dried thyme
- Salt and pepper to taste

Spinach and Strawberry Salad
Ingredients:

- 4 cups baby spinach leaves
- 1 cup sliced strawberries

- 1/4 cup sliced almonds
- 2 tablespoons balsamic vinaigrette dressing

Preparation Time: 1 hour

Method:

1. In a large pot, heat olive oil over medium heat. Add beef stew meat and cook until browned on all sides. Remove meat from the pot and set aside.
2. In the same pot, add diced onion, carrots, and celery. Cook until softened, about 5 minutes.
3. Add minced garlic and cook for an additional minute.

4. Return browned beef stew meat to the pot. Pour in beef broth and bring to a boil. Add pearl barley, diced tomatoes, chopped spinach, and dried thyme. Simmer for 45 minutes, or until beef and barley are tender.

5. Season with salt and pepper to taste.

6. While the soup is simmering, prepare the spinach and strawberry salad by combining baby spinach leaves, sliced strawberries, and sliced almonds in a large bowl.

7. Drizzle balsamic vinaigrette dressing over the salad and toss until well coated.

8. Serve the beef and barley soup hot, accompanied by the spinach and strawberry salad.

4. Lentil Soup with Mediterranean Chickpea Salad

Lentil Soup Ingredients:

- 2 tablespoons olive oil
- 1 onion, diced
- 2 carrots, diced
- 2 celery stalks, diced
- 3 cloves garlic, minced
- 1 cup dried green or brown lentils, rinsed
- 6 cups vegetable broth
- 1 can (14 oz) diced tomatoes
- 1 teaspoon ground cumin

- 1 teaspoon ground coriander
- Salt and pepper to taste

Mediterranean Chickpea Salad
Ingredients:

- 1 can (15 oz) chickpeas, drained and rinsed
- 1 cucumber, diced
- 1/2 cup cherry tomatoes, halved
- 1/4 cup diced red onion
- 1/4 cup chopped fresh parsley
- 2 tablespoons extra virgin olive oil
- 1 tablespoon lemon juice
- 1 teaspoon dried oregano
- Salt and pepper to taste

Preparation Time: 1 hour

Method:

1. In a large pot, heat olive oil over medium heat. Add diced onion, carrots, and celery. Cook until softened, about 5 minutes.
2. Add minced garlic and cook for an additional 2 minute.
3. Add rinsed lentils, vegetable broth, diced tomatoes, ground cumin, and ground coriander to the pot. Bring to a boil, then reduce heat and simmer for 30-40 minutes, or until lentils are tender.
4. Season with salt and pepper to taste.
5. While the soup is simmering, prepare the Mediterranean chickpea salad by combining

drained and rinsed chickpeas, diced cucumber, halved cherry tomatoes, diced red onion, and chopped fresh parsley in a large bowl.

6. In a small bowl, whisk together extra virgin olive oil, lemon juice, dried oregano, salt, and pepper to make the dressing.

7. Drizzle the dressing over the salad and toss until well combined.

8. Serve the lentil soup hot, accompanied by the Mediterranean chickpea salad.

5. Thai Coconut Curry Soup with Crunchy Asian Salad

Thai Coconut Curry Soup Ingredients:

- 2 tablespoons coconut oil
- 1 onion, diced
- 2 cloves garlic, minced
- 2 tablespoons Thai red curry paste
- 4 cups vegetable broth
- 1 can (14 oz) coconut milk
- 2 cups chopped mixed vegetables (such as bell peppers, broccoli, and snow peas)
- 1 cup cooked rice noodles or rice vermicelli
- 2 tablespoons soy sauce or tamari
- 1 tablespoon lime juice
- Salt and pepper to taste

- Fresh cilantro for garnish (optional)

Crunchy Asian Salad Ingredients:

- 4 cups shredded cabbage (green or purple)
- 1 carrot, grated
- 1/4 cup chopped fresh cilantro
- 1/4 cup chopped peanuts or cashews
- 2 tablespoons rice vinegar
- 1 tablespoon sesame oil
- 1 teaspoon honey or maple syrup
- Salt and pepper to taste

Preparation Time: 45 minutes

Method:

1. In a large pot, heat coconut oil over medium heat. Add diced onion and cook until softened, about 5 minutes.
2. Add minced garlic and Thai red curry paste to the pot. Cook for an additional minute.
3. Pour in vegetable broth and coconut milk. Bring to a simmer.
4. Add chopped mixed vegetables to the pot and simmer for 10-15 minutes, or until vegetables are tender.
5. Stir in cooked rice noodles or rice vermicelli, soy sauce or tamari, and lime juice. Cook for another 2-3 minutes.

6. Season with salt and pepper to taste. Garnish with fresh cilantro if desired.
7. While the soup is simmering, prepare the Crunchy Asian Salad by combining shredded cabbage, grated carrot, chopped fresh cilantro, and chopped peanuts or cashews in a large bowl.
8. In a small bowl, whisk together rice vinegar, sesame oil, honey or maple syrup, salt, and pepper to make the dressing.
9. Drizzle the dressing over the salad and toss until well combined.
10. Serve the Thai Coconut Curry Soup hot, accompanied by the Crunchy Asian Salad.

11. These hearty and filling soup-salad combos offer a delightful mix of flavors and textures, making them perfect for a satisfying and nutritious meal. Enjoy the delicious taste of each dish and feel good knowing you're nourishing your body with wholesome ingredients.

Salad

Chapter 6: Appetizing Appetizers and Snacks

Here, we explore a variety of appetizing appetizers and snacks that are perfect for satisfying cravings between meals or for entertaining guests. From crispy veggie chips and dips to protein-packed snack bites and flavorful low-carb dippers, these recipes are both delicious and nutritious, making them ideal for any occasion.

Crispy Veggie Chips and Dips

1 Baked Zucchini Chips

Ingredients:

- 2 medium zucchinis, thinly sliced

- 2 tablespoons olive oil
- 1/4 cup grated Parmesan cheese
- 1 teaspoon garlic powder
- 1 teaspoon dried thyme
- Salt and pepper to taste

Preparation Time: 25 minutes

Method:

1. Preheat the oven to 400°F (200°C). Line a baking sheet with parchment paper.
2. In a large bowl, toss the thinly sliced zucchinis with olive oil until evenly coated.
3. In a separate bowl, combine grated Parmesan cheese, garlic

powder, dried thyme, salt, and pepper.

4. Dip each zucchini slice into the Parmesan mixture, coating both sides evenly, and place them on the prepared baking sheet in a single layer.

5. Bake for 20-25 minutes, flipping halfway through, until the zucchini chips are golden brown and crispy.

6. Remove from the oven and leave to cool slightly then serve. Enjoy with your favorite dip, such as tzatziki or ranch dressing.

2 Crispy Kale Chips

Ingredients:

- A bunch kale, with it's stems removed and torn into tiny or bite-sized pieces
- 1 tablespoon olive oil
- 1 teaspoon smoked paprika
- 1/2 teaspoon garlic powder
- Salt to taste

Preparation Time: 20 minutes

Method:

1. Preheat the oven to 350°F (175°C). Line a baking sheet with parchment paper.
2. In a large bowl, toss the kale pieces with olive oil until evenly coated.

3. Sprinkle smoked paprika, garlic powder, and salt over the kale and toss again to coat evenly.
4. Spread the seasoned kale pieces out in a single layer on the prepared baking sheet.
5. Bake for 10-15 minutes, or until the kale chips are crispy and lightly browned around the edges.
6. Remove from the oven and let to cool before you serve. Enjoy as a crunchy and nutritious snack on their own or with your favorite dip.

.3 Baked Sweet Potato Chips

Ingredients:

- 2 medium sweet potatoes, thinly sliced
- 2 tablespoons olive oil
- 1 teaspoon smoked paprika
- 1/2 teaspoon garlic powder
- Salt to taste

Preparation Time: 30 minutes

Method:

1. Preheat the oven to 400°F (200°C). Line a baking sheet with parchment paper.
2. In a large bowl, toss the thinly sliced sweet potatoes with olive oil until evenly coated.
3. Sprinkle smoked paprika, garlic powder, and salt over the sweet

potatoes and toss again to coat evenly.

4. Spread the seasoned sweet potato slices out in a single layer on the prepared baking sheet.

5. Bake for 25-30 minutes, flipping halfway through, until the sweet potato chips are crispy and golden brown.

6. Remove from the oven and let cool slightly before serving. Enjoy with your favorite dip, such as hummus or guacamole.

.4 Baked Beet Chips

Ingredients:

2 large beets, peeled and thinly sliced

2 tablespoons olive oil

1 teaspoon garlic powder

1/2 teaspoon smoked paprika

Salt and pepper to taste

Preparation Time: 30 minutes

Method:

Preheat the oven to 350°F (175°C). Line a baking sheet with parchment paper.

In a large bowl, toss the thinly sliced beets with olive oil until evenly coated.

Sprinkle garlic powder, smoked paprika, salt, and pepper over the beets and toss again to coat evenly.

Spread the seasoned beet slices out in a single layer on the prepared baking sheet.

Bake for 20-25 minutes, flipping halfway through, until the beet chips are crispy and lightly browned.

Remove from the oven and let cool slightly before serving. Enjoy with your favorite dip, such as hummus or tzatziki.

5 Crispy Parmesan Cauliflower Bites

Ingredients:

1 head cauliflower, cut into florets

1/2 cup grated Parmesan cheese

1/4 cup almond flour

1 teaspoon garlic powder

1/2 teaspoon dried oregano

1/2 teaspoon smoked paprika

Salt and pepper to taste

2 eggs, beaten

Preparation Time: 30 minutes

Method:

Preheat the oven to 400°F (200°C). Line a baking sheet with parchment paper.

In a shallow bowl, combine grated Parmesan cheese, almond flour, garlic powder, dried oregano, smoked paprika, salt, and pepper.

Dip each cauliflower floret into the beaten eggs, then coat with the Parmesan mixture, pressing gently to adhere.

Place the coated cauliflower florets on the prepared baking sheet in a single layer.

Bake in the preheated oven for 20-25 minutes, or until the cauliflower bites are golden brown and crispy.

Remove from the oven and let cool slightly before serving.

Serve the crispy Parmesan cauliflower bites hot, with marinara sauce or ranch dressing for dipping.

Protein-Packed Snack Bites

1 Almond Butter Energy Balls

Ingredients:

- 1 cup rolled oats
- 1/2 cup almond butter
- 1/4 cup honey or maple syrup
- 1/4 cup chopped almonds
- 1/4 cup mini chocolate chips
- 1 teaspoon vanilla extract
- Pinch of salt

Preparation Time: 15 minutes

Method:

1. In a large bowl, combine rolled oats, almond butter, honey or maple syrup, chopped almonds, mini chocolate chips, vanilla extract, and a pinch of salt.
2. Mix till well combined and the mixture holds together.
3. Roll the mixture into small balls,, and place them on a baking sheet lined with parchment paper.
4. Allow to chill in the refrigerator for at least 30 minutes to firm up.
5. Once firm, transfer the almond butter energy balls to an airtight container and store in the refrigerator until ready to serve. Enjoy as a protein-packed snack on the go or as a post-workout treat.

.2 Turkey and Cheese Roll-Ups

Ingredients:

- 4 slices turkey breast
- 4 slices cheddar cheese
- 1/2 avocado, sliced
- 1/2 cucumber, julienned
- 1/4 cup baby spinach leaves

Preparation Time: 10 minutes

Method:

1. Lay a slice of turkey breast flat on a cutting board. Place a slice of cheddar cheese on top.

2. Layer sliced avocado, julienned cucumber, and baby spinach leaves on top of the cheese.
3. Roll up the turkey slice tightly, enclosing the filling.
4. Repeat with the remaining turkey slices and filling ingredients.
5. Secure each roll-up with a toothpick if necessary.
6. Serve immediately as a protein-packed snack or appetizer.

.3 Greek Yogurt Parfait

Ingredients:

- 1 cup Greek yogurt
- 1/4 cup granola

- Quarter ¼ cup of mixed berries like; strawberries, blueberries, and raspberries
- Drizzle of honey or maple syrup (optional)

Preparation Time: 5 minutes

Method:

1. In a bowl, layer the Greek yogurt, granola, and them mixed berries.
2. Repeat the layers until all ingredients are used, ending with a layer of mixed berries on top.
3. Drizzle honey or maple syrup over the top if you like.

4. Serve immediately as a protein-packed snack or light and refreshing dessert.

4 Peanut Butter Banana Oat Bites

Ingredients:

1 ripe banana, mashed

1/2 cup creamy peanut butter

1 cup rolled oats

1/4 cup mini chocolate chips

1/4 cup chopped nuts (such as almonds or walnuts)

1 tablespoon honey or maple syrup

Pinch of salt

Preparation Time: 15 minutes

Method:

In a medium bowl, combine mashed banana, creamy peanut butter, rolled oats, mini chocolate chips, chopped nuts, honey or maple syrup, and a pinch of salt.

Mix well to combine the mixture so it holds together.

Roll the mixture into small balls, and place on a baking sheet lined with parchment paper.

Allow to Chill in the refrigerator for at least 30 minutes to firm up.

Once firm, transfer the peanut butter banana oat bites to an airtight container and store in the refrigerator until ready to serve.

Enjoy as a protein-packed snack or as a sweet treat.

.5 Smoked Salmon Cucumber Bites

Ingredients:

1 English cucumber, cut into rounds

4 oz smoked salmon,have it cut into bite-size pieces

1/4 cup cream cheese

2 tablespoons capers

Fresh dill for garnish

Preparation Time: 10 minutes

Method:

Spread a thin layer of cream cheese on each cucumber .

Top each cucumber round with a piece of smoked salmon.

Garnish with capers and fresh dill.

Serve immediately as a protein-packed snack or elegant appetizer.

6.3 Flavorful Low Carb Dippers

6.3.4 Bacon-Wrapped Asparagus Spears

Ingredients:

1 bunch asparagus, trimmed

8 slices bacon

1 tablespoon olive oil

Salt and pepper to taste

Preparation Time: 25 minutes

Method:

Preheat the oven to 400°F (200°C). Line a baking sheet with parchment paper.

Drizzle olive oil over the trimmed asparagus spears and season with salt and pepper.

163

Wrap each asparagus spear with a slice of bacon, starting from the bottom and wrapping it tightly to the top.

Place the bacon-wrapped asparagus spears on the prepared baking sheet.

Bake in the preheated oven for 20-25 minutes, or until the bacon is crispy and the asparagus is tender.

Remove from the oven and let cool and serve.

Serve the bacon-wrapped asparagus spears hot, with your favorite dipping sauce.

Flavorful Low Carb Dippers

1 Cucumber Chips with Tzatziki

Ingredients:

- 2 large cucumbers, thinly sliced
- 1 cup Greek yogurt
- 1/2 cucumber, grated and drained
- 2 cloves garlic, minced
- 1 tablespoon fresh lemon juice
- 1 tablespoon chopped fresh dill
- Salt and pepper to taste

Preparation Time: 20 minutes

Method:

1. In a medium bowl, combine Greek yogurt, grated cucumber, minced garlic, lemon juice, chopped fresh dill, salt, and pepper. Stir until well combined.
2. Cover and refrigerate the tzatziki sauce for at least 30 minutes to allow the flavors to meld.
3. Arrange the thinly sliced cucumbers on a serving platter.
4. Serve the cucumber chips with the chilled tzatziki sauce for dipping.

2 Bell Pepper Nachos

Ingredients:

- 2 large bell peppers,with seeds removed and halved

- 1/2 lb ground beef or turkey
- 1 tablespoon taco seasoning
- 1/2 cup shredded cheddar cheese
- 1/4 cup diced tomatoes
- 1/4 cup sliced black olives
- 2 tablespoons chopped fresh cilantro
- Sour cream and guacamole for serving

Preparation Time: 30 minutes

Method:

1. Preheat the oven to 375°F (190°C). Line a baking sheet with parchment paper.

2. Place the halved bell peppers on the prepared baking sheet, cut side up.
3. In a skillet cook the ground beef or turkey under medium heat until browned and cooked through. Drain any excess fat.
4. Add taco seasoning to the skillet and stir to combine with the cooked meat.
5. Spoon the seasoned meat mixture into each bell pepper half.
6. Top each bell pepper half with shredded cheddar cheese, diced tomatoes, and sliced black olives.
7. Bake in oven for 15-20 minutes, preferably until the cheese is melted and bubbly.

8. Take it out from the oven and garnish with freshly chopped cilantro.

9. Serve the bell pepper nachos hot, with sour cream and guacamole on the side for dipping.

3 Parmesan Zucchini Fries

Ingredients:

- 2 large zucchinis, cut into sticks
- 1/2 cup grated Parmesan cheese
- 1/4 cup almond flour
- 1 teaspoon garlic powder
- 1 teaspoon dried oregano
- 1/2 teaspoon paprika
- Salt and pepper to taste
- 2 eggs, beaten

Preparation Time: 30 minutes

Method:

1. Preheat the oven to 425°F
   (220°C). Line a baking sheet with
   parchment paper.
2. In a shallow bowl, combine grated
   Parmesan cheese, almond flour,
   garlic powder, dried oregano,
   paprika, salt, and pepper.
3. Dip each zucchini stick into the
   beaten eggs, then coat with the
   Parmesan mixture, pressing gently
   to adhere.
4. Place the coated zucchini sticks on
   the prepared baking sheet in a
   single layer.

5. Bake in the preheated oven for 15-20 minutes, or until the zucchini fries are golden brown and crispy.
6. Take it out from the oven and let cool slightly before serving plates.
7. Serve the Parmesan zucchini fries hot, with marinara sauce or ranch dressing for dipping.

4 Bacon-Wrapped Asparagus Spears

Ingredients:

1 bunch asparagus, trimmed

8 slices bacon

1 tablespoon olive oil

Salt and pepper to taste

Preparation Time: 25 minutes

Method:

Preheat the oven to 400°F (200°C). Line a baking sheet with parchment paper.

Drizzle olive oil over the trimmed asparagus spears and season with salt and pepper.

Wrap each asparagus spear with a slice of bacon, starting from the bottom and wrapping it tightly to the top.

Place the bacon-wrapped asparagus spears on the prepared baking sheet.

Bake in the preheated oven for 20-25 minutes, or until the bacon is crispy and the asparagus is tender.

Remove from the oven and let cool slightly before serving.

Serve the bacon-wrapped asparagus spears hot, with your favorite dipping sauce.

5 Cheese-Stuffed Mini Bell Peppers

Ingredients:

12 mini bell peppers, halved and seeds removed

1 cup shredded cheese (such as cheddar or mozzarella)

1/4 cup chopped fresh parsley

1 teaspoon garlic powder

Salt and pepper to taste

Preparation Time: 20 minutes

Method:

Preheat the oven to 375°F (190°C). Line a baking sheet with parchment paper.

In a small bowl, mix together shredded cheese, chopped fresh parsley, garlic powder, salt, and pepper.

Stuff each mini bell pepper half with the cheese mixture.

Place the stuffed mini bell peppers on the prepared baking sheet.

Bake in a preheated oven for 15-20 minutes, until the cheese is melted and bubbly.

Remove from the oven and let cool slightly before serving.

Serve the cheese-stuffed mini bell peppers hot, with salsa or guacamole for dipping.

These appetizing appetizers and snacks offer a wide range of flavors and textures to satisfy any craving. Whether you're in the mood for something crunchy, protein-packed, or flavorful, these recipes are sure to delight your taste buds and keep you feeling satisfied between meals. Enjoy these delicious and nutritious snacks on their own or as part of a larger spread for entertaining guests.

Chapter 7: Mouthwatering Main Dishes

In Chapter 7, we delve into a world of mouthwatering main dishes that are sure to become family favorites. From savory seafood specialties to delectable poultry pleasures, these recipes are packed with flavor and easy to prepare. Let's explore five simple recipes for each category:

Savory Seafood Specialties

1 Lemon Garlic Shrimp Scampi

Ingredients:

- 1 lb large shrimp, peeled and deveined
- 4 cloves garlic, minced
- 2 tablespoons olive oil
- 2 tablespoons unsalted butter
- 1/4 cup fresh lemon juice
- Zest of 1 lemon
- 1/4 cup chopped fresh parsley
- Salt and pepper to taste
- Cooked pasta or crusty bread for serving (optional)

Preparation Time: 15 minutes

Method:

1. Heat up olive oil and butter in a large skillet over low-medium heat.
2. Add minced garlic to the skillet and cook until fragrant, about 1 minute.
3. Add shrimp to the skillet and cook until pink and opaque, for about 2-3 minutes on each side.
4. Stir in fresh lemon juice and lemon zest, then season with salt and pepper to taste.
5. Remove from heat and sprinkle chopped fresh parsley over the shrimp.
6. Serve the lemon garlic shrimp scampi hot, over cooked pasta or

with crusty bread for soaking up
the flavorful sauce.

2 Baked Salmon with Dill Sauce

Ingredients:

- 4 salmon fillets
- 2 tablespoons olive oil
- Salt and pepper to taste
- 1/4 cup plain Greek yogurt
- 1 tablespoon chopped fresh dill
- 1 tablespoon Dijon mustard
- 1 tablespoon lemon juice
- 1 clove garlic, minced

Preparation Time: 25 minutes

Method:

1. Preheat the oven to 400°F (200°C). Line a baking sheet with parchment paper.
2. Place salmon fillets on the prepared baking sheet and drizzle with olive oil. Season with salt and pepper.
3. Bake in the preheated oven for 12-15 minutes, or until salmon is cooked through and flakes easily with a fork.
4. While the salmon is baking, prepare the dill sauce by combining Greek yogurt, chopped fresh dill, Dijon mustard, lemon juice, and minced garlic in a small bowl. Stir until well combined.
5. Serve the baked salmon hot, with a dollop of dill sauce on top.

3 Garlic Butter Shrimp Pasta

Ingredients:

- 8 oz linguine or spaghetti
- 1 lb large shrimp, peeled and deveined
- 4 cloves garlic, minced
- 4 tablespoons unsalted butter
- 1/4 cup chopped fresh parsley
- Salt and pepper to taste
- Grated Parmesan cheese for serving (optional)

Preparation Time: 20 minutes

Method:

1. Cook pasta according to package instructions until al dente. Drain and set aside.
2. In a skillet, melt butter. Add minced garlic and cook until fragrant.
3. Now,add shrimp to the skillet and cook until pink and opaque, about 2-3 minutes on each side.
4. Toss cooked pasta with the garlic butter shrimp in the skillet, then sprinkle chopped fresh parsley over the top.
5. Season with salt and pepper to taste.
6. Serve the garlic butter shrimp pasta hot, with grated Parmesan cheese on top if desired.

.4 Grilled Lemon Herb Tilapia

Ingredients:

- 4 tilapia fillets
- 2 tablespoons olive oil
- 2 tablespoons fresh lemon juice
- 1 teaspoon lemon zest
- 1 teaspoon chopped fresh thyme
- 1 teaspoon chopped fresh parsley
- Salt and pepper to taste
- Lemon wedges for serving

Preparation Time: 15 minutes

Method:

1. Preheat grill to medium-high heat.

2. In a small bowl, whisk together olive oil, lemon juice, lemon zest, chopped fresh thyme, chopped fresh parsley, salt, and pepper.
3. Brush both sides of tilapia fillets with the lemon herb mixture.
4. Place tilapia fillets on the preheated grill and cook for 3-4 minutes per side, or until fish is opaque and flakes easily with a fork.
5. Remove from grill and serve the grilled lemon herb tilapia hot, with lemon wedges on the side.

.5 Spicy Cajun Shrimp and Sausage Skillet

Ingredients:

- 1 lb large shrimp, peeled and deveined
- 8 oz smoked sausage, sliced
- 1 bell pepper, diced
- 1 onion, diced
- 3 cloves garlic, minced
- 2 tablespoons Cajun seasoning
- 2 tablespoons olive oil
- Cooked rice for serving

Preparation Time: 20 minutes

Method:

1. Heat up the olive oil in a large skillet over medium-high heat.
2. Add diced bell pepper and onion to the skillet and cook until softened, about 5 minutes.

3. Add minced garlic and Cajun seasoning to the skillet and cook for an additional minute.
4. Add sliced smoked sausage to the skillet and cook until browned, about 3-4 minutes.
5. Stir in shrimp and cook until pink and opaque, about 2-3 minutes per side.
6. Serve the spicy Cajun shrimp and sausage skillet hot, over cooked rice.

Delectable Poultry Pleasures

.1 Garlic Herb Roast Chicken

Ingredients:

- 1 whole chicken (about 4 lbs), giblets removed
- 4 tablespoons unsalted butter, softened
- 4 cloves garlic, minced
- 1 tablespoon chopped fresh rosemary
- 1 tablespoon chopped fresh thyme

- Salt and pepper to taste
- 1 lemon, halved

Preparation Time: 1 hour 30 minutes

Method:

1. Preheat the oven to 425°F (220°C). Line the entire roasting pan with aluminum foil.
2. In a small bowl, mix together softened butter, minced garlic, chopped fresh rosemary, chopped fresh thyme, salt, and pepper.
3. Pat the whole chicken dry with paper towels, then rub the garlic herb butter mixture all over the chicken, including under the skin.

4. Place the lemon halves inside the cavity of the chicken.

5. Bind the chicken legs together with kitchen twine and tuck the wing tips under the body .

6. Place the prepared chicken in the roasting pan and roast in the preheated oven for 1 hour to 1 hour 15 minutes, or until the internal temperature reaches 165°F (75°C) and the skin is golden brown and crispy.

7. Take out from the oven and let rest for 10 minutes before carving.

8. Serve the garlic herb roast chicken hot, with your favorite side dishes.

2 Baked Honey Mustard Chicken

Ingredients:

- 4 boneless, skinless chicken breasts
- 1/4 cup Dijon mustard
- 2 tablespoons honey
- 1 tablespoon olive oil
- 2 cloves garlic, minced
- Salt and pepper to taste
- Chopped fresh parsley for garnish

Preparation Time: 30 minutes

Method:

1. Preheat the oven to 400°F (200°C). Line the baking dish with parchment paper.
2. In a small bowl, whisk together Dijon mustard, honey, olive oil, minced garlic, salt, and pepper.
3. Place chicken breasts in the prepared baking dish and brush with the honey mustard mixture, coating both sides evenly.
4. Bake in the preheated oven for 20-25 minutes, or until chicken is cooked through and juices run clear.
5. Take out from the oven and let to rest for 5 minutes before serving.
6. Garnish with chopped fresh parsley and serve the baked honey

mustard chicken hot, with your favorite side dishes.

3 Lemon Herb Grilled Chicken

Ingredients:

- 4 boneless, skinless chicken breasts
- 1/4 cup olive oil
- 2 tablespoons fresh lemon juice
- 1 tablespoon chopped fresh thyme
- 1 tablespoon chopped fresh rosemary
- 2 cloves garlic, minced
- Salt and pepper to taste
- Lemon wedges for serving

Preparation Time: 25 minutes

Method:

1. In a small bowl, whisk together olive oil, lemon juice, chopped fresh thyme, chopped fresh rosemary, minced garlic, salt, and pepper.
2. Place chicken breasts in a shallow dish or resealable plastic bag and pour the lemon herb marinade over the chicken. Ensure all pieces are evenly coated. Marinate in the refrigerator for 30 minutes, preferably up to 4 hours.
3. Preheat grill to medium-high heat.
4. Remove chicken from marinade and discard excess marinade.

5. Grill chicken breasts for 6-8 minutes per side, or until cooked through and juices run clear.
6. Remove from grill, let it rest for 5 minutes and then serve.
7. Serve the lemon herb grilled chicken hot, with lemon wedges on the side for squeezing over the top.

4 Creamy Mushroom Chicken Skillet

Ingredients:

- 4 boneless, skinless chicken breasts
- Salt and pepper to taste
- 2 tablespoons olive oil
- 8 oz mushrooms, sliced

- 2 cloves garlic, minced
- 1 cup chicken broth
- 1/2 cup heavy cream
- 1 tablespoon chopped fresh parsley

Preparation Time: 30 minutes

Method:

1. Season chicken breasts with salt and pepper to taste.
2. Heat olive oil in a large skillet. Add chicken breasts to the skillet and cook for 6-8 minutes per side, or until browned and cooked through. Remove the chicken from the skillet and set it aside.

3. In that same skillet, add some sliced mushrooms and minced garlic. Cook until mushrooms are golden brown and tender, about 5 minutes.

4. Pour chicken broth into the skillet and bring to a simmer, scraping up any browned bits from the bottom of the skillet.

5. Stir in heavy cream and return chicken breasts to the skillet. Simmer for another 5 minutes, or until sauce has thickened slightly and chicken is heated through.

6. Sprinkle some chopped fresh parsley over the top before serving if you like.

7. Serve the creamy mushroom chicken hot, with your favorite side dishes.

5 Spinach and Feta Stuffed Chicken Breast

Ingredients:

- 4 boneless, skinless chicken breasts
- Salt and pepper to taste
- 1 cup baby spinach leaves
- 1/2 cup crumbled feta cheese
- 2 cloves garlic, minced
- 1 tablespoon olive oil
- Toothpicks

Preparation Time: 35 minutes

Method:

1. Preheat the oven to 375°F (190°C). Line baking dish with some parchment paper.
2. Place each chicken breast between two sheets of plastic wrap and pound to an even thickness using a meat mallet or rolling pin. Season with salt and pepper to taste.
3. In a small bowl, combine baby spinach leaves, crumbled feta cheese, and minced garlic.
4. Divide the spinach and feta mixture evenly among the chicken breasts, spooning it onto one side of each breast.

5. Roll up each chicken breast tightly, enclosing the filling, and secure with toothpicks.

6. Heat olive oil in a skillet over medium-heat. Add rolled chicken breasts to the skillet and cook until browned on all sides, about 2-3 minutes per side.

7. Transfer browned chicken breasts to the prepared baking dish and bake in the preheated oven for 20-25 minutes, or until chicken is cooked through and juices run clear.

8. Remove from the oven and let rest for 7 minutes before serving.

9. Serve the spinach and feta stuffed chicken breast hot, with your favorite side dishes.

These mouthwatering main dishes are perfect for any occasion, from weeknight dinners to special gatherings with family and friends. With simple ingredients and easy-to-follow instructions, you'll be able to whip up these delicious recipes in no time. Enjoy the savory seafood specialties and delectable poultry pleasures, and savor every bite!

Flavorful Meaty Marvels

1 Beef and Broccoli Stir-Fry

Ingredients:

- 1 lb flank steak, thinly sliced
- 1/4 cup soy sauce
- 2 tablespoons oyster sauce
- 1 tablespoon cornstarch
- 2 tablespoons vegetable oil
- 4 cups broccoli florets
- 3 cloves garlic, minced
- 1 tablespoon fresh ginger, grated
- Cooked rice for serving

Preparation Time: 25 minutes

Method:

1. In a bowl, mix soy sauce, oyster sauce, and cornstarch to create the marinade.
2. Toss sliced flank steak in the marinade and let it sit for 15 minutes.
3. Heat vegetable oil in a wok over high heat. Add marinated beef and stir-fry until browned.
4. Add broccoli florets, minced garlic, and grated ginger. Continue to stir-fry until broccoli is tender-crisp.
5. Serve the beef and broccoli stir-fry hot over cooked rice.

.2 Classic Spaghetti Bolognese

Ingredients:

- 1 lb ground beef
- 1 onion, finely chopped
- 2 cloves garlic, minced
- 1 carrot, grated
- 1 celery stalk, finely chopped
- 1 can (28 oz) crushed tomatoes
- 1/2 cup red wine (optional)
- 2 tablespoons tomato paste
- 1 teaspoon dried oregano
- Salt and pepper to taste
- Cooked spaghetti for serving

Preparation Time: 40 minutes

Method:

1. In a skillet, brown ground beef over medium heat. Drain excess fat.

2. Add chopped onion, minced garlic, grated carrot, and chopped celery to the skillet. Cook until vegetables are softened.
3. Stir in crushed tomatoes, red wine (if using), tomato paste, dried oregano, salt, and pepper. Simmer for 20-25 minutes.
4. Serve the classic spaghetti Bolognese over cooked spaghetti.

3 Honey Garlic Glazed Chicken Thighs

Ingredients:

- 4 bone-in, skin-on chicken thighs
- Salt and pepper to taste
- 1/4 cup honey

- 3 tablespoons soy sauce
- 2 tablespoons ketchup
- 2 cloves garlic, minced
- 1 teaspoon fresh ginger, grated
- Sesame seeds and chopped green onions.
- Cooked rice for serving

Preparation Time: 35 minutes

Method:

1. Preheat the oven to 400°F (200°C). Season chicken thighs with salt and pepper.
2. In a bowl, whisk together honey, soy sauce, ketchup, minced garlic, and grated ginger.

3. Place chicken thighs in a baking dish and brush them with the honey garlic glaze.
4. Bake in the preheated oven for 25-30 minutes, or until chicken is cooked through and skin is crispy.
5. Garnish with sesame seeds and chopped green onions. Serve the honey garlic glazed chicken thighs hot over cooked rice.

.4 Pork Carnitas Tacos

Ingredients:

- 2 lbs pork shoulder, cut into chunks
- 1 onion, sliced
- 4 cloves garlic, minced

- 1 teaspoon ground cumin
- 1 teaspoon dried oregano
- 1 teaspoon smoked paprika
- Salt and pepper to taste
- 1 orange, juiced
- Corn tortillas for serving
- For garnish fresh cilantro,lime wedges and diced onions.

Preparation Time: 3 hours (including slow cooking)

Method:

1. Season pork chunks with cumin, dried oregano, smoked paprika, salt, and pepper.
2. Place seasoned pork, sliced onion, and minced garlic in a slow

cooker. Pour orange juice over the top.

3. Cook on low for 6-8 hours or until pork is tender and can be easily shredded.

4. Shred the pork using two forks and spread it on a baking sheet. Broil for 5 minutes until edges are crispy.

5. Serve the pork carnitas in corn tortillas with fresh cilantro, diced onions, and lime wedges.

5 Teriyaki Glazed Salmon

Ingredients:

- 4 salmon fillets
- 1/4 cup soy sauce

- 2 tablespoons mirin
- 2 tablespoons sake (or white wine)
- 2 tablespoons brown sugar
- 1 tablespoon vegetable oil
- 1 teaspoon fresh ginger, grated
- 1 clove garlic, minced
- Sesame seeds and sliced green onions
- Cooked rice for serving

Preparation Time: 20 minutes

Method:

1. In a bowl, whisk together soy sauce, mirin, sake, brown sugar, grated ginger, and minced garlic to make the teriyaki sauce.

2. Heat vegetable oil in a skillet over medium-high heat. Sear salmon fillets for 2-3 minutes on each side

Vegetarian and Vegan Varieties

.1 Spaghetti Aglio e Olio

Ingredients:

- 8 oz spaghetti
- 4 cloves garlic, thinly sliced
- 1/4 cup extra virgin olive oil
- 1/2 teaspoon red pepper flakes
- 1/4 cup chopped fresh parsley
- Salt to taste

Preparation Time: 15 minutes

Method:

1. Cook spaghetti according to package instructions until al dente. Drain and set aside.
2. In a large skillet, heat olive oil over medium heat. Add thinly sliced garlic and red pepper flakes. Cook until garlic is golden brown and fragrant, about 2-3 minutes.
3. Add cooked spaghetti to the skillet and toss to coat with the garlic-infused oil.
4. Season with salt to taste and sprinkle chopped fresh parsley over the top.
5. Serve the spaghetti aglio e olio hot, garnished with additional red

pepper flakes and grated
Parmesan cheese if desired.

2 Chickpea Curry

Ingredients:

- 2 tablespoons vegetable oil
- 1 onion, diced
- 3 cloves garlic, minced
- 1 tablespoon grated ginger
- 2 tablespoons curry powder
- 1 teaspoon ground cumin
- 1 teaspoon ground coriander
- 1/2 teaspoon turmeric
- 1 can (15 oz) chickpeas, drained and rinsed
- 1 can (14 oz) coconut milk
- 1 cup vegetable broth

- Salt and pepper to taste
- Cooked rice or naan for serving

Preparation Time: 30 minutes

Method:

1. Heat vegetable oil in a large skillet over medium heat. Add diced onion, minced garlic, and grated ginger. Cook until onion is soft and translucent, about 5 minutes.
2. Stir in curry powder, ground cumin, ground coriander, and turmeric. Cook for another minute until fragrant.
3. Add drained chickpeas, coconut milk, and vegetable broth to the skillet. Bring to a simmer and cook

for 15-20 minutes, stirring occasionally, until the sauce thickens.

4. Season with salt and pepper to taste.

5. Serve the chickpea curry hot over cooked rice or with naan bread on the side.

3 Lentil Shepherd's Pie

Ingredients:

- 2 cups cooked lentils
- 1 onion, diced
- 2 carrots, diced
- 2 cloves garlic, minced
- 1 cup frozen peas
- 1 cup vegetable broth

- 2 tablespoons tomato paste
- 2 tablespoons soy sauce
- 1 tablespoon olive oil
- Mashed potatoes for topping

Preparation Time: 45 minutes

Method:

1. Preheat the oven to 375°F (190°C). Lightly grease a baking dish.
2. Heat olive oil in a large skillet over medium heat. Add diced onion, diced carrots, and minced garlic. Cook until vegetables are softened, about 5-7 minutes.
3. Stir in cooked lentils, frozen peas, vegetable broth, tomato paste, and soy sauce. Simmer for 10-15

minutes until the mixture thickens slightly.

4. Transfer the lentil mixture to the prepared baking dish. Spread mashed potatoes evenly over the top.

5. Bake in the preheated oven for 25-30 minutes, or until the mashed potatoes are golden brown and the filling is bubbly.

6. Serve the lentil shepherd's pie hot, garnished with chopped fresh parsley if desired.

4 Mushroom Stroganoff

Ingredients:

- 8 oz egg noodles

- 2 tablespoons olive oil
- 1 onion, diced
- 8 oz cremini mushrooms, sliced
- 2 cloves garlic, minced
- 1 tablespoon all-purpose flour
- 1 cup vegetable broth
- 1 cup sour cream (or dairy-free alternative)
- 2 tablespoons Worcestershire sauce (or vegan alternative)
- Salt and pepper to taste
- Chopped fresh parsley for garnish

Preparation Time: 25 minutes

Method:

1. Cook egg noodles according to package instructions until al dente. Drain and set aside.
2. Heat olive oil in a large skillet over medium heat. Add diced onion and sliced mushrooms. Cook until mushrooms are golden brown and onions are softened, about 5-7 minutes.
3. Add minced garlic to the skillet and cook for another minute until fragrant.
4. Sprinkle all-purpose flour over the mushroom mixture and stir to coat evenly. Cook for 1-2 minutes to remove the raw flour taste.
5. Slowly pour in vegetable broth, stirring constantly to prevent lumps from forming. Bring to a

simmer and cook until the sauce thickens, about 5 minutes.

6. Stir in sour cream and Worcestershire sauce. Season with salt and pepper to taste.

7. Serve the mushroom stroganoff hot over cooked egg noodles, garnished with chopped fresh parsley.

5 Vegan Eggplant Parmesan

Ingredients:

- 1 large eggplant, sliced into rounds
- 1 cup all-purpose flour
- 1 cup breadcrumbs (or almond meal for a gluten-free option)
- 1 cup marinara sauce

- 1 cup vegan mozzarella cheese, shredded
- 1/4 cup nutritional yeast
- Fresh basil leaves for garnish
- Olive oil for frying

Preparation Time: 40 minutes

Method:

1. Preheat the oven to 375°F (190°C). Lightly grease a baking dish.
2. Dredge eggplant slices in flour, then dip them into breadcrumbs to coat evenly.
3. Heat olive oil in a large skillet over medium-high heat. Fry breaded eggplant slices until golden brown

and crispy, about 3-4 minutes per side. Drain on paper towels.

4. Spread a thin layer of marinara sauce in the bottom of the prepared baking dish. Place fried eggplant slices on top.

5. Sprinkle vegan mozzarella cheese and nutritional yeast over the eggplant slices.

6. Bake in the preheated oven for 20-25 minutes, or until the cheese is melted and bubbly.

7. Serve the vegan eggplant Parmesan hot, garnished with fresh basil leaves.

These vegetarian and vegan main dishes showcase the versatility and deliciousness of plant-based cooking.

Whether you're following a meatless diet or simply looking to incorporate more plant-based meals into your routine, these recipes are sure to satisfy your taste buds and leave you feeling satisfied and nourished. Enjoy exploring the flavors and textures of these mouthwatering dishes!

ENJOY!!!

Chapter 8: Sides and Accompaniments

In Chapter 8, we explore a variety of side dishes and accompaniments that perfectly complement our main dishes. From low-carb veggie sides to wholesome grain alternatives, these recipes add flavor and nutrition to any meal. Let's dive into five simple recipes for each category:

Low Carb Veggie Sides

.1 Garlic Parmesan Roasted Asparagus

Ingredients:

- 1 lb asparagus spears, trimmed
- 2 tablespoons olive oil
- 2 cloves garlic, minced
- 1/4 cup grated Parmesan cheese
- Salt and pepper to taste
- Lemon wedges for serving (optional)

Preparation Time: 20 minutes

Method:

1. Preheat the oven to 400°F (200°C). Line a baking sheet with parchment paper.
2. Place trimmed asparagus spears on the prepared baking sheet.
3. Drizzle olive oil over the asparagus and sprinkle minced garlic, grated Parmesan cheese, salt, and pepper evenly.
4. Toss the asparagus so it coats evenly with the seasoning
5. Roast in the preheated oven for 12-15 minutes, or until the asparagus is tender and lightly browned.
6. Serve the garlic Parmesan roasted asparagus hot, with lemon wedges on the side if desired.

.2 Cauliflower Mash

Ingredients:

- 1 head cauliflower, chopped into florets
- 2 cloves garlic, minced
- 2 tablespoons butter or olive oil
- Salt and pepper to taste
- Chopped fresh chives for garnish (optional)

Preparation Time: 20 minutes

Method:

1. Steam or boil cauliflower florets until tender, about 8-10 minutes.

2. Drain the cauliflower with a sieve and transfer it to a food processor of your choice

3. Add minced garlic, butter or olive oil, salt, and pepper to the food processor.

4. Pulse until the cauliflower is smooth and creamy, scraping down the sides as needed.

5. Transfer the cauliflower mash to a serving bowl and garnish with chopped fresh chives if desired.

6. Serve the cauliflower mash hot, as a low-carb alternative to mashed potatoes.

3 Zucchini Noodles (Zoodles)

Ingredients:

- 2 medium zucchini
- 1 tablespoon olive oil
- Salt and pepper to taste
- Fresh basil leaves for garnish (optional)

Preparation Time: 10 minutes

Method:

1. Using a vegetable peeler, create zucchini noodles (zoodles).
2. Heat olive oil in a skillet over medium heat.
3. Add zucchini noodles to the skillet and cook for 2-3 minutes, tossing occasionally, until tender.
4. Season with salt and pepper to taste.

5. Garnish with fresh basil leaves if desired.

6. Serve the zucchini noodles hot, as a low-carb alternative to pasta.

4 Roasted Brussels Sprouts

Ingredients:

- 1 lb Brussels sprouts, trimmed and halved
- 2 tablespoons olive oil
- 2 cloves garlic, minced
- Salt and pepper to taste
- Balsamic glaze for drizzling (optional)

Preparation Time: 25 minutes

Method:

1. Preheat the oven to 400°F (200°C). Line a baking sheet with parchment paper.
2. Place trimmed and halved Brussels sprouts on the prepared baking sheet.
3. Drizzle olive oil over the Brussels sprouts and sprinkle minced garlic, salt, and pepper evenly.
4. Toss the Brussels sprouts to coat evenly with the seasonings.
5. Roast in the oven for 20-25 minutes, until the Brussels sprouts are tender and caramelised.
6. If you desire, drizzle with balsamic glaze before serving.

5 Creamy Spinach and Mushroom Saute

Ingredients:

- 8 oz baby spinach
- 8 oz cremini mushrooms, sliced
- 2 cloves garlic, minced
- 2 tablespoons butter or olive oil
- Quarter of a cup of heavy cream (or coconut cream for a dairy-free option)
- Salt and pepper to taste
- Grated Parmesan cheese for garnish (optional)

Preparation Time: 15 minutes

Method:

1. Heat butter or olive oil in a skillet.
2. Add sliced cremini mushrooms to the skillet and cook until golden brown and tender, about 5-7 minutes.
3. Add minced garlic to the skillet and cook for another minute until fragrant.
4. Stir in baby spinach and cook until wilted, about 2-3 minutes.
5. Pour in heavy cream (or coconut cream) and simmer until the sauce thickens slightly.
6. Season with salt and pepper to taste.
7. Serve the creamy spinach and mushroom saute hot, garnished with grated Parmesan cheese if desired.

Wholesome Grain Alternatives

.1 Quinoa Pilaf

Ingredients:

- 1 cup quinoa, rinsed
- 2 cups vegetable broth
- 1 tablespoon olive oil
- 1 onion, diced
- 2 cloves garlic, minced
- 1/4 cup chopped fresh parsley
- Salt and pepper to taste

Preparation Time: 20 minutes

Method:

1. In a saucepan, heat olive oil over medium heat. Add diced onion and minced garlic. Cook until onion is soft and about 3- 5 minutes.
2. Add rinsed quinoa to the saucepan and toast for 2-3 minutes, stirring occasionally.
3. Pour in vegetable broth and allow to boil. Reduce heat,cover, and simmer for 15 minutes, until quinoa is cooked and liquid is absorbed.
4. Fluff quinoa with a fork and stir in chopped fresh parsley.
5. Season with salt and pepper to taste.

6. Serve the quinoa pilaf hot, as a wholesome grain alternative to rice or pasta.

.2 Cauliflower Rice

Ingredients:

- 1 head cauliflower, chopped into florets
- 2 tablespoons olive oil
- 2 cloves garlic, minced
- Salt and pepper to taste
- Chopped fresh cilantro for garnish (optional)

Preparation Time: 15 minutes

Method:

1. Place cauliflower florets in a food processor and pulse until they resemble rice grains.
2. Heat up olive oil in large skillet over medium heat. Add minced garlic and cook until fragrant.
3. Add cauliflower rice to the skillet and cook for 5-7 minutes, stirring occasionally, until tender.
4. Season with salt and pepper to taste.
5. Garnish with chopped fresh cilantro if desired.
6. Serve the cauliflower rice hot, as a wholesome grain alternative to traditional rice.

3 Broccoli Rice

Ingredients:

- 1 head broccoli, chopped into florets
- 2 tablespoons olive oil
- 2 cloves garlic, minced
- Salt and pepper to taste
- Lemon zest for garnish (optional)

Preparation Time: 15 minutes

Method:

1. Place broccoli florets in a food processor and pulse until they resemble rice grains.
2. Heat olive oil in a large skillet. Add the minced garlic and cook until fragrant.

3. Add broccoli rice to the skillet and cook for 5-7 minutes, stirring occasionally, until tender.
4. Season with salt and pepper to taste.
5. Garnish with lemon zest if desired.
6. Serve the broccoli rice hot, as a wholesome grain alternative to traditional rice.

4 Spaghetti Squash with Marinara Sauce

Ingredients:

- 1 spaghetti squash
- 2 cups marinara sauce (store-bought or homemade)
- 1 tablespoon olive oil

- Salt and pepper to taste
- Fresh basil leaves for garnish (optional)

Preparation Time: 45 minutes

Method:

1. Preheat the oven to 400°F (200°C). Cut spaghetti squash in half lengthwise and scoop out the seeds.
2. Drizzle olive oil over the cut sides of the spaghetti squash and season with salt and pepper.
3. Place spaghetti squash halves cut-side down on a baking sheet lined with parchment paper.

4. Roast in the preheated oven for 35-40 minutes, or until the flesh is tender and easily pierced with a fork.
5. Scrape the flesh of the spaghetti squash with a fork to create spaghetti-like strands.
6. Heat marinara sauce in a saucepan over medium heat until warmed through.
7. Serve the roasted spaghetti squash topped with marinara sauce and garnished with fresh basil leaves if desired.

5 Baked Sweet Potato Fries

Ingredients:

- 2 sweet potatoes, peeled and cut into fries
- 2 tablespoons olive oil
- 1 teaspoon smoked paprika
- 1 teaspoon garlic powder
- Salt and pepper to taste
- Fresh parsley for garnish (optional)

Preparation Time: 30 minutes

Method:

1. Preheat the oven to 425°F (220°C). Line a baking sheet with parchment paper.
2. In a large bowl, toss sweet potato fries with olive oil, smoked

paprika, garlic powder, salt, and
pepper until evenly coated.

3. Spread sweet potato fries in a
   single layer on the prepared
   baking sheet, ensuring they are
   not crowded.
4. Bake in the preheated oven for 25-
   30 minutes, flipping halfway
   through, until fries are crispy and
   golden brown.
5. Garnish with fresh parsley if
   desired.
6. Serve the baked sweet potato fries
   hot, as a wholesome grain
   alternative to traditional potato
   fries.

These side dishes and accompaniments
are perfect for rounding out any meal,

whether you're serving a hearty main course or a light salad. With simple ingredients and easy-to-follow instructions, you can elevate your dining experience and enjoy wholesome and delicious dishes every time.

Savory Sauce and Dressing Recipes

.1 Classic Marinara Sauce

Ingredients:

- 2 tablespoons olive oil
- 1 onion, diced
- 3 cloves garlic, minced
- 1 can (28 oz) crushed tomatoes
- 1 teaspoon dried oregano

- 1 teaspoon dried basil
- Salt and pepper to taste
- Fresh basil leaves for garnish (optional)

Preparation Time: 30 minutes

Method:

1. Heat olive oil in a saucepan. Add diced onion and minced garlic. Cook until onion is soft and translucent.
2. Stir in crushed tomatoes, dried oregano, and dried basil. Season with salt and pepper to taste.
3. Bring the sauce to a simmer and cook for 20-25 minutes, stirring occasionally, until thickened.

4. Garnish with fresh basil leaves if desired.

5. Serve the classic marinara sauce hot over pasta, pizza, or as a dipping sauce for breadsticks.

2 Creamy Garlic Parmesan Sauce

Ingredients:

- 2 tablespoons butter
- 3 cloves garlic, minced
- 1 cup heavy cream
- 1/2 cup grated Parmesan cheese
- Salt and pepper to taste
- Chopped fresh parsley for garnish (optional)

Preparation Time: 15 minutes

Method:

1. Melt butter in a saucepan over medium heat. Add minced garlic and cook until fragrant.
2. Pour in heavy cream and bring to a simmer.
3. Reduce heat to low and stir in grated Parmesan cheese until melted and smooth.
4. Season with salt and pepper to taste.
5. Simmer for 6 minutes or until the sauce thickens slightly.
6. Garnish with chopped fresh parsley if desired.
7. Serve the creamy garlic Parmesan sauce hot over pasta, chicken, or vegetables.

.3 Tangy Balsamic Vinaigrette

Ingredients:

- 1/4 cup balsamic vinegar
- 1/4 cup olive oil
- 1 tablespoon Dijon mustard
- 1 clove garlic, minced
- 1 teaspoon honey (optional)
- Salt and pepper to taste

Preparation Time: 5 minutes

Method:

1. In a small bowl, whisk together balsamic vinegar, olive oil, Dijon mustard, minced garlic, and honey (if using) until well combined.

2. Season with salt and pepper to taste.
3. Store in an airtight container in the refrigerator until you want to use.
4. Shake well before serving.
5. Serve the tangy balsamic vinaigrette over salads, grilled vegetables, or as a marinade for meats.

4 Spicy Sriracha Mayo

Ingredients:

- 1/2 cup mayonnaise
- 2 tablespoons Sriracha sauce
- 1 tablespoon lime juice
- 1 teaspoon honey (optional)

- Salt to taste

Preparation Time: 5 minutes

Method:

1. In a small bowl, whisk together mayonnaise, Sriracha sauce, lime juice, and honey (if using) until smooth.
2. Season with salt to taste.
3. Adjust the amount of Sriracha sauce according to your desired level of spiciness.
4. Store in an airtight container in the refrigerator until use.
5. Serve the spicy Sriracha mayo as a dipping sauce for fries, seafood, or sandwiches.

5 Lemon Herb Dressing

Ingredients:

- 1/4 cup olive oil
- 2 tablespoons lemon juice
- 1 teaspoon Dijon mustard
- 1 teaspoon honey (optional)
- 1 clove garlic, minced
- 1 tablespoon chopped fresh herbs (such as parsley, basil, or thyme)
- Salt and pepper to taste

Preparation Time: 5 minutes

Method:

1. In a small bowl, whisk together olive oil, lemon juice, Dijon

mustard, honey (if using), minced garlic, chopped fresh herbs, salt, and pepper until well combined.

2. Adjust the amount of lemon juice and honey according to your taste preferences.

3. Store in an airtight container in the refrigerator till you want to use.

4. Shake well before serving.

5. Serve the lemon herb dressing over salads, grilled chicken, or roasted vegetables.

These savory sauces and dressings are versatile additions to your culinary repertoire, adding depth and complexity to your favorite dishes. Whether you prefer a classic marinara sauce, a creamy garlic Parmesan sauce, or a tangy balsamic vinaigrette, there's something here for everyone to enjoy. Experiment with different flavors and ingredients to customize these recipes to suit your taste preferences and elevate your meals to new heights of deliciousness.

Chapter 9: Sweet Endings

In Chapter 9, we explore a world of delectable desserts that are both satisfying and mindful of your health goals. From decadent low-carb creations to guilt-free indulgences, these recipes will delight your taste buds without compromising your commitment to wellness.

Decadent Low Carb Desserts

Indulge in the rich flavors and luxurious textures of these low-carb desserts that are sure to satisfy your sweet tooth without derailing your diet.

.1 Chocolate Avocado Mousse

Ingredients:

- 2 ripe avocados
- 1/4 cup unsweetened cocoa powder
- Quarter cup of sugar-free sweetener (example:erythritol or stevia)
- 1 teaspoon vanilla extract
- Pinch of salt
- Optional toppings: whipped cream, shaved dark chocolate

Preparation Time: 10 minutes

Method:

1. Scoop the flesh of the avocados into a food processor.
2. Add cocoa powder, sugar-free sweetener, vanilla extract, and a pinch of salt.
3. Blend until smooth and creamy.
4. Taste and adjust sweetness if necessary.
5. Transfer the mousse into serving bowls .
6. Allow to sit in the refrigerator for at least 30 minutes before you serve.
7. Garnish with whipped cream and shaved dark chocolate if desired.

2 Keto Cheesecake Bites

Ingredients:

- 8 oz cream cheese, softened
- 1/4 cup sugar-free sweetener (such as erythritol or monk fruit)
- 1 large egg
- 1 teaspoon vanilla extract
- Optional toppings: sugar-free fruit preserves, whipped cream

Preparation Time: 20 minutes

Method:

1. Preheat the oven to 325°F (160°C). Line a mini muffin tin with paper liners.
2. In a mixing bowl, beat cream cheese and sugar-free sweetener until smooth.

3. Add egg and vanilla extract, and beat until well combined.

4. Spoon the mixture into the prepared mini muffin tin, filling each cavity about 2/3 full.

5. Bake for 15-18 minutes, or until the cheesecake bites are set but still slightly jiggly in the center.

6. Remove from the oven and let cool in the muffin tin for 10 minutes.

7. Transfer to a rack to cool.

8. Once cooled, refrigerate for at least 2 hours before you serve.

9. Top with sugar-free fruit preserves or whipped cream before serving if desired.

3 Coconut Flour Brownies

Ingredients:

- 1/2 cup coconut flour
- 1/2 cup unsweetened cocoa powder
- 1/2 cup sugar-free sweetener (such as erythritol or stevia)
- 1/2 teaspoon baking powder
- Pinch of salt
- 1/2 cup coconut oil, melted
- 4 large eggs
- 1 teaspoon vanilla extract
- Optional add-ins: chopped nuts, sugar-free chocolate chips

Preparation Time: 30 minutes

Method:

1. Preheat the oven to 350°F (175°C). Grease an 8x8-inch baking pan or

preferably,line it with parchment paper.

2. In a mixing bowl, whisk together coconut flour, cocoa powder, sugar-free sweetener, baking powder, and salt.

3. Add melted coconut oil, eggs, and vanilla extract to the dry ingredients. Mix until well combined.

4. If using, fold in chopped nuts or sugar-free chocolate chips.

5. Pour the batter into the prepared baking pan and spread it out.

6. Bake for 20-25 minutes, or until the edges are set and a toothpick inserted into the center comes out with a few moist crumbs.

7. Let cool completely in the pan before slicing into squares.

8. Serve these coconut flour brownies as a delicious low-carb dessert option.

4 Peanut Butter Chocolate Fat Bombs

Ingredients:

- 1/2 cup creamy peanut butter
- 1/4 cup coconut oil, melted
- 2 tablespoons unsweetened cocoa powder
- 2 tablespoons sugar-free sweetener (such as erythritol or stevia)
- Pinch of salt

Preparation Time: 10 minutes

Method:

1. In a mixing bowl, combine creamy peanut butter, melted coconut oil, cocoa powder, sugar-free sweetener, and a pinch of salt. Mix until smooth.
2. Spoon the mixture into silicone candy molds or mini muffin cups, filling each about halfway.
3. Freeze for 1-2 hours, or until firm.
4. Once firm, pop the fat bombs out of the molds or muffin cups.
5. Store in an airtight container in the freezer until ready to eat and enjoy..
6. These peanut butter chocolate fat bombs are perfect for a quick

energy boost or a satisfying dessert.

5 Vanilla Chia Seed Pudding

Ingredients:

- 1/4 cup chia seeds
- 1 cup unsweetened almond milk (or any milk of choice)
- 1 tablespoon sugar-free sweetener (such as erythritol or stevia)
- 1 teaspoon vanilla extract
- Optional toppings: fresh berries, sliced almonds, unsweetened coconut flakes

Preparation Time: 5 minutes (plus chilling time)

Method:

1. In a mixing bowl or mason jar, whisk together chia seeds, almond milk, sugar-free sweetener, and vanilla extract.
2. Cover and refrigerate for at least 2 hours, or overnight, until the mixture thickens into a pudding-like consistency.
3. Stir the chia seed pudding before serving to evenly distribute the seeds.
4. Top with fresh berries, sliced almonds, or unsweetened coconut flakes for added flavor and texture.
5. Serve this vanilla chia seed pudding as a satisfying and nutritious low-carb dessert option.

Guilt-Free Treats and Indulgences

Satisfy your cravings for something sweet with these guilt-free treats and indulgences that are lighter on calories but still bursting with flavor.

1 Fruit Salad with Honey Lime Dressing

Ingredients:

- Assorted fresh fruits (such as strawberries, blueberries, pineapple, and kiwi), chopped
- 2 tablespoons fresh lime juice
- 1 tablespoon honey or maple syrup for a vegiterian)

- Fresh mint leaves for garnish (optional)

Preparation Time: 15 minutes

Method:

1. In a large bowl, combine chopped fresh fruits.
2. In a small bowl, whisk together fresh lime juice and honey until well combined.
3. Pour the honey lime dressing over the fruit salad and gently toss to coat.
4. Garnish with fresh mint leaves before serving if desired.

5. Serve this refreshing fruit salad as a guilt-free dessert or snack option.

2 Greek Yogurt Parfait

Ingredients:

- Plain Greek yogurt
- Fresh berries (such as strawberries, blueberries, raspberries)
- Granola (look for a low-sugar or preferably sugar-free bar)
- Optional toppings: honey, nuts, shredded coconut

Preparation Time: 5 minutes

Method:

1. In a glass or parfait dish, layer plain Greek yogurt, fresh berries, and granola.
2. Repeat them layers until the glass is filled or to your liking.
3. Drizzle honey over the top if desired and sprinkle with nuts or shredded coconut for added crunch.
4. Serve this Greek yogurt parfait as a nutritious and satisfying dessert or breakfast option.

3 Frozen Banana Bites

Ingredients:

- Ripe bananas, peeled and sliced into rounds
- Smooth peanut butter or almond butter
- Dark chocolate chips
- Optional toppings: shredded coconut, chopped nuts, sea salt

Preparation Time: 30 minutes (plus freezing time)

Method:

1. Spread peanut butter or almond butter on one side of each banana slice.
2. Sandwich two banana slices together, with the nut butter in the middle, to form a bite-sized treat.

3. Place the banana bites on a parchment-lined baking sheet and freeze for 15-20 minutes, or until firm.

4. Melt dark chocolate chips in the microwave or over a double boiler until smooth.

5. Dip each frozen banana bite into the melted chocolate, coating it halfway.

6. Place the chocolate-covered banana bites back on the baking sheet and sprinkle with shredded coconut, chopped nuts, or a pinch of sea salt if desired.

7. Return the baking sheet to the freezer and freeze until the chocolate is set.

8. Serve these frozen banana bites as a satisfying and nutritious dessert or snack option.

4 Berry Coconut Popsicles

Ingredients:

- Assorted fresh berries, strawberries, blueberries and raspberries
- Unsweetened coconut milk
- Optional add-ins: honey, vanilla extract, shredded coconut

Preparation Time: 5 minutes (plus freezing time)

Method:

1. Place fresh berries into popsicle molds, filling each mold about halfway.
2. Pour coconut milk over the berries until the molds are filled to the top.
3. If desired, sweeten the coconut milk with honey and add a splash of vanilla extract for extra flavor.
4. Use a popsicle stick to gently stir the mixture and distribute the berries evenly.
5. Insert popsicle sticks into the molds and freeze for at least 4 hours, or until solid.
6. Once it is frozen, run the molds under warm water for a 10 seconds to release the popsicles.

7. Serve these berry coconut popsicles as a refreshing and wholesome dessert or snack option.

5 Almond Butter Energy Balls

Ingredients:

- 1 cup rolled oats
- 1/2 cup almond butter
- 1/4 cup honeyor maple syrup.
- 1/4 cup dark chocolate chips
- 1/4 cup chopped nuts ,almonds, walnuts, or pecans)
- Optional add-ins: chia seeds, flaxseeds, shredded coconut

Preparation Time: 15 minutes (plus chilling time)

Method:

1. In a mixing bowl, combine rolled oats, almond butter, honey, dark chocolate chips, and chopped nuts.
2. If desired, add in additional add-ins such as chia seeds, flaxseeds, or shredded coconut for extra nutrition and flavor.
3. Stir until all ingredients are well combined and form a sticky dough.
4. Roll the dough into small balls using your clean hands.
5. Place the energy balls on a parchment-lined baking sheet and

chill in the refrigerator for at least
30 minutes to firm up.

6. Once chilled, transfer the energy
   balls to an airtight container and
   store in the refrigerator until ready
   to enjoy.

7. These almond butter energy balls
   make a convenient and nutritious
   on-the-go snack or a guilt-free
   dessert option.

With these decadent low-carb desserts
and guilt-free treats and indulgences,
you can satisfy your sweet cravings while
staying on track with your health goals.
Experiment with different flavors and
ingredients to customize these recipes to
your liking, and enjoy the delicious
results guilt-free.

Creative Low Carb Baking

Get ready to unleash your inner baker and explore the possibilities of low-carb ingredients with these delightful recipes.

1 Almond Flour Chocolate Chip Cookies

Ingredients:

- 2 cups almond flour
- 1/2 cup sugar-free sweetener (erythritol or stevia)
- 1/2 teaspoon baking soda
- 1/4 teaspoon salt
- 1/3 cup coconut oil, melted

- 1 large egg
- 1 teaspoon vanilla extract
- 1/2 cup sugar-free chocolate chips

Preparation Time: 15 minutes

Cook Time: 10-12 minutes

Total Time: 25-27 minutes

Method:

1. Preheat the oven to 350°F (175°C). Line a baking sheet with parchment paper.
2. In a mixing bowl, combine almond flour, sugar-free sweetener, baking soda, and salt.
3. Add melted coconut oil, egg, and vanilla extract to the dry

ingredients. Mix until well combined.

4. Fold in sugar-free chocolate chips until evenly distributed throughout the dough.

5. Usin a tablespoon take sized portions of dough onto the baking sheet, spacing them few inches apart.

6. Flatten the dough balls slightly with the palm of your hand.

7. Bake until the edges are golden brown.

8. Let it cool on the baking sheet for 5 minutes, then transfer to a rack to cool completely.

9. Enjoy these almond flour chocolate chip cookies as a

satisfying and low-carb dessert or snack option.

.2 Coconut Flour Lemon Cake

Ingredients:

- 1/2 cup coconut flour
- 1/2 cup sugar-free sweetener (erythritol or stevia)
- 1 teaspoon baking powder
- 1/4 teaspoon salt
- 1/3 cup coconut oil, melted
- 4 large eggs
- 1/4 cup unsweetened almond milk
- Zest and juice of 1 lemon
- 1 teaspoon vanilla extract

Preparation Time: 15 minutes

Cook Time: 25-30 minutes

Total Time: 40-45 minutes

Method:

1. Preheat the oven to 350°F (175°C). Grease a 9x9-inch baking pan or line it with parchment paper.
2. In a mixing bowl, whisk together coconut flour, sugar-free sweetener, baking powder, and salt.
3. In a separate bowl, whisk together melted coconut oil, eggs, almond milk, lemon zest, lemon juice, and vanilla extract.
4. Add the wet ingredients to the dry ingredients and mix well

5. Pour the batter into the prepared baking pan and spread .

6. Bake for 25-30 minutes, until toothpick inserted into the center comes out smoothly and clean.

7. Let cool in the pan for 10 minutes, then transfer to a wire rack.

8. Serve slices of this coconut flour lemon cake as a delightful low-carb dessert option.

.3 Zucchini Bread with Walnuts

Ingredients:

- 2 cups almond flour
- 1/2 cup coconut flour
- 1/2 cup sugar-free sweetener (erythritol or stevia)

- 1 teaspoon baking powder
- 1 teaspoon baking soda
- 1/2 teaspoon salt
- 1 teaspoon ground cinnamon
- 4 large eggs
- 1/3 cup coconut oil, melted
- 1/4 cup unsweetened almond milk
- 2 cups grated zucchini
- 1/2 cup chopped walnuts

Preparation Time: 15 minutes

Cook Time: 40-45 minutes

Total Time: 55-60 minutes

Method:

1. Preheat the oven to 350°F (175°C). Grease a 9x5-inch loaf pan.

2. In a mixing bowl, combine almond flour, coconut flour, sugar-free sweetener, baking powder, baking soda, salt, and ground cinnamon.

3. In a separate bowl, whisk together eggs, melted coconut oil, and almond milk.

4. Add the wet ingredients to the dry ingredients and mix well.

5. Fold in grated zucchini and chopped walnuts until evenly distributed throughout the batter.

6. Pour the batter into the prepared loaf pan.

7. Bake until a toothpick inserted into the center comes out clean.

8. Let cool in the pan for 5 minutes, then transfer to a rack to cool completely.

9. Slice and serve this zucchini bread with walnuts as a nutritious and flavorful low-carb dessert or snack option.

4 Pumpkin Spice Muffins

Ingredients:

- 1 cup almond flour
- 1/4 cup coconut flour
- 1/2 cup sugar-free sweetener (erythritol or stevia)
- 1 teaspoon baking powder
- 1/2 teaspoon baking soda
- 1/2 teaspoon salt
- 1 teaspoon ground cinnamon
- 1/2 teaspoon ground ginger
- 1/4 teaspoon ground nutmeg

- 1/4 teaspoon ground cloves
- 1/2 cup pumpkin puree
- 1/3 cup coconut oil, melted
- 1/4 cup unsweetened almond milk
- 2 large eggs
- 1 teaspoon vanilla extract

Preparation Time: 15 minutes

Cook Time: 20-22 minutes

Total Time: 35-37 minutes

Method:

1. Preheat the oven to 350°F (175°C). Line a muffin tin with paper liners.
2. In a mixing bowl, whisk together almond flour, coconut flour, sugar-free sweetener, baking

powder, baking soda, salt, and spices.

3. In a separate bowl, whisk together pumpkin puree, melted coconut oil, almond milk, eggs, and vanilla extract.

4. Add the wet ingredients to the dry ingredients and mix.

5. Spoon the batter into the prepared muffin tin, filling each cup about 2/3 full.

6. Bake for 20-22 minutes, preferably a toothpick inserted into the center should come out clean.

7. Let cool in the muffin tin for 5 minutes, then transfer to a rack to cool.

8. Enjoy these pumpkin spice muffins as a delicious and seasonal low-carb treat.

5 Chocolate Avocado Brownies

Ingredients:

- 2 ripe avocados
- 1/2 cup unsweetened cocoa powder
- 1/2 cup sugar-free sweetener (erythritol or stevia)
- 2 large eggs
- 1 teaspoon vanilla extract
- 1/4 cup almond flour
- 1/4 teaspoon baking soda
- Pinch of salt
- 1/4 cup sugar-free chocolate chips

Preparation Time: 15 minutes

Cook Time: 25-30 minutes

Total Time: 40-45 minutes

Method:

1. Preheat the oven to 350°F (175°C). an 8x8-inch baking dish should be lined with parchment paper.
2. Scoop the flesh of the avocados into a food processor or your blender.
3. Add cocoa powder, sugar-free sweetener, eggs, and vanilla extract to the blender. Blend until smooth.

4. In a mixing bowl, combine almond flour, baking soda, and a pinch of salt.

5. Pour the avocado mixture into the dry ingredients and mix until well combined.

6. Fold in sugar-free chocolate chips.

7. Pour the batter into the baking dish evenly.

8. Bake for 25-30 minutes, or until the edges are set and a toothpick inserted into the center comes out clean.

9. Let cool in the baking dish for 10 minutes, then transfer to a wire rack to cool completely.

10. Slice and serve these chocolate avocado brownies as a rich and fudgy low-carb dessert option.

With these creative low-carb baking recipes, you can enjoy delicious treats while staying true to your dietary goals. Experiment with different flavors and ingredients to customize these recipes to your liking, and delight in the guilt-free pleasure of homemade sweets.

Chapter 10: Drinks and Beverages

Quench your thirst and elevate your beverage game with a selection of refreshing drinks and cocktails designed to complement your low-carb lifestyle.

Hydrating Infusions and Teas

Stay hydrated and invigorated with these hydrating infusions and teas, perfect for any time of day.

1 Citrus Mint Infused Water

Ingredients:

- 1 lemon, sliced

- 1 lime, sliced
- Handful of fresh mint leaves
- 6 cups water
- Ice cubes (optional)

Preparation Time: 5 minutes (plus chilling time)

Method:

1. In a large pitcher, combine lemon slices, lime slices, and fresh mint leaves.
2. Pour water over the ingredients and stir gently to combine.
3. Cover the pitcher and refrigerate for an hour or more to allow the flavors to com alive.
4. Serve over ice cubes if desired.

5. Enjoy this refreshing citrus mint infused water as a hydrating and flavorful beverage.

2 Berry Hibiscus Iced Tea

Ingredients:

- 4 cups water
- 4 hibiscus tea bags
- 1 cup mixed berries, strawberries, and blueberries,raspberries,
- 1-2 tablespoons sugar-free sweetener (optional)
- Ice cubes

Preparation Time: 10 minutes (plus chilling time)

Method:

1. Boil water in a medium saucepan.
2. Remove from heat and add hibiscus tea bags. Let steep for 5-7 minutes.
3. Remove tea bags and discard.
4. Add mixed berries and sugar-free sweetener (if using) to the tea, stirring until sweetener is dissolved.
5. Allow the tea to cool to room temperature, then refrigerate until chilled.
6. Serve over ice cubes and garnish with additional berries if desired.
7. Enjoy this vibrant and fruity berry hibiscus iced tea as a refreshing low-carb beverage option.

3 Cucumber Basil Spa Water

Ingredients:

- 1 cucumber, thinly sliced
- Handful of fresh basil leaves
- 6 cups water
- Ice cubes (optional)

Preparation Time: 5 minutes (plus chilling time)

Method:

1. In a large pitcher, combine cucumber slices and fresh basil leaves.
2. Pour water over the ingredients and stir gently to combine.

3. Cover the pitcher and refrigerate for at least an hour or more to allow the flavors infuse.
4. Serve over ice cubes if desired.
5. Enjoy this rejuvenating cucumber basil spa water as a hydrating and aromatic beverage.

10.1.4 Ginger Turmeric Wellness Tea

Ingredients:

- 4 cups water
- 2 teaspoons grated fresh ginger
- 1 teaspoon ground turmeric
- 1-2 tablespoons lemon juice
- 1-2 tablespoons honey or sugar-free sweetener (optional)

Preparation Time: 10 minutes

Method:

1. In saucepan, bring water to a simmer.
2. Add grated ginger and ground turmeric to the simmering water.
3. Let the mixture steep for 5-7 minutes.
4. Remove from heat and strain out the ginger and turmeric.
5. Stir in lemon juice and honey or sugar-free sweetener to taste.
6. Serve hot and enjoy this invigorating ginger turmeric wellness tea as a soothing and healthful beverage.

.5 Green Tea with Mint and Lemon

Ingredients:

- 4 cups water
- 4 green tea bags
- Handful of fresh mint leaves
- 1 lemon, sliced
- Ice cubes (optional)

Preparation Time: 5 minutes (plus chilling time)

Method:

1. Bring water to a boil in a medium saucepan.
2. Remove from heat and add green tea bags. Let steep for 3-5 minutes.

3. Remove tea bags and discard.

4. Add fresh mint leaves and lemon slices to the tea, stirring gently.

5. Allow the tea to cool to room temp, then keep in the refrigerator until chilled.

6. Serve over ice cubes if desired.

7. Enjoy this revitalizing green tea with mint and lemon as a refreshing and antioxidant-rich beverage.

Low Carb Cocktails and Mocktails

Raise a toast to good times with these low-carb cocktails and mocktails that are big on flavor but light on carbs.

.1 Keto Mojito Mocktail

Ingredients:

- 1 tablespoon fresh lime juice
- 2 teaspoons sugar-free sweetener
- Handful of fresh mint leaves
- 1/2 cup club soda
- Ice cubes
- Lime wedges and additional mint leaves for garnish

Preparation Time: 5 minutes

Method:

1. In a glass, muddle fresh lime juice, sugar-free sweetener, and mint leaves together.

2. Fill the glass with ice cubes.

3. Top with club soda and stir gently to combine.

4. Garnish with lime wedges and additional mint leaves.

5. Enjoy this refreshing keto mojito mocktail as a guilt-free alternative to the classic cocktail.

2 Skinny Margarita

Ingredients:

- 2 oz tequila
- 1 oz fresh lime juice
- 1 oz orange liqueur (such as triple sec or Cointreau)
- Lime wedge for garnish
- Salt for rimming (optional)

Preparation Time: 5 minutes

Method:

1. Rim a glass with salt (if desired) by running a lime wedge around the rim and dipping it into salt.
2. Fill the glass with ice cubes.
3. In a cocktail shaker, combine tequila, fresh lime juice, and orange liqueur.
4. Shake very well and strain into the glass.
5. Garnish with a lime wedge.
6. Enjoy this light and refreshing skinny margarita as a low-carb cocktail option.

3 Berry Sparkler Mocktail

Ingredients:

- 1/4 cup of mixed berries like strawberries, raspberries, and blueberries.
- 1 tablespoon sugar-free sweetener
- 1/2 cup sparkling water or club soda
- Ice cubes
- Lemon or lime wedges for garnish

Preparation Time: 5 minutes

Method:

1. In a glass, muddle mixed berries with sugar-free sweetener until well combined.
2. Fill the glass with ice cubes.

3. Pour sparkling water , preferably club soda over the berries.
4. Stir gently to combine.
5. Garnish with lemon or lime wedges.
6. Enjoy this refreshing berry sparkler mocktail as a vibrant and flavorful beverage option.

4 Vodka Soda with Lime

Ingredients:

- 1 1/2 oz vodka
- 3 oz soda water
- Fresh lime wedge for garnish
- Ice cubes

Preparation Time: 5 minutes

Method:

1. Fill a glass with ice cubes.
2. Pour vodka over the ice.
3. Top with soda water.
4. Stir gently to combine.
5. Garnish with a fresh lime wedge.
6. Enjoy this classic vodka soda with lime as a simple and low-carb cocktail option.

5 Coconut Lime Mocktail

Ingredients:

- 1/2 cup coconut water
- 2 tablespoons fresh lime juice
- 1 tablespoon sugar-free sweetener
- Splash of coconut milk (optional)

- Lime wedge for garnish
- Ice cubes

Preparation Time: 5 minutes

Method:

1. Fill a glass with ice cubes.
2. In a separate glass, combine coconut water, fresh lime juice, and sugar-free sweetener.
3. Stir until sweetener is dissolved.
4. Pour the mixture over the ice cubes.
5. Add a splash of coconut milk if desired.
6. Garnish with a lime wedge.

7. Enjoy this tropical coconut lime mocktail as a refreshing and hydrating beverage option.

With these creative and flavorful low-carb drinks and beverages, you can enjoy a wide variety of refreshing options while staying true to your dietary goals. Experiment with different ingredients and flavors to customize these recipes to your liking, and toast to good health with every sip.

Energizing Smoothie and Shake Recipes

Start your day or refuel after a workout with these delicious and nutritious smoothie and shake recipes.

.1 Berry Blast Smoothie

Ingredients:

- 1 cup mixed berries (strawberries, blueberries, raspberries)
- 1/2 banana, frozen
- 1/2 cup spinach
- 1/2 cup unsweetened almond milk
- 1/4 cup Greek yogurt (optional)
- 1 tablespoon chia seeds (optional)

- Ice cubes

Preparation Time: 5 minutes

Method:

1. Combine all ingredients in a blender.
2. Blend until smooth and creamy.
3. Pour into a glass and enjoy immediately.

.2 Green Goddess Smoothie

Ingredients:

- 1 cup spinach
- 1/2 cucumber, chopped
- 1/2 avocado

- 1/2 cup pineapple chunks
- 1 tablespoon fresh ginger, grated
- 1 tablespoon lime juice
- 1/2 cup coconut water
- Ice cubes

Preparation Time: 5 minutes

Method:

1. Place all ingredients in a blender.
2. Blend until smooth and creamy.
3. Pour into a glass and serve immediately.

3 Chocolate Peanut Butter Protein Shake

Ingredients:

- 1 scoop chocolate protein powder
- 1 tablespoon unsweetened cocoa powder
- 1 tablespoon natural peanut butter
- 1/2 banana, frozen
- 1 cup unsweetened almond milk
- Ice cubes

Preparation Time: 5 minutes

Method:

1. Add all ingredients to a blender.
2. Blend until smooth and creamy.
3. Pour into a glass and enjoy immediately.

4 Tropical Paradise Smoothie

Ingredients:

- 1/2 cup frozen mango chunks
- 1/2 cup frozen pineapple chunks
- 1/2 banana, frozen
- 1/2 cup coconut water
- 1/4 cup Greek yogurt (optional)
- 1 tablespoon honey or maple syrup (optional)
- Ice cubes

Preparation Time: 5 minutes

Method:

1. Combine all ingredients in a blender.
2. Blend until smooth and creamy.

3. Pour into a glass and serve immediately.

.5 Vanilla Almond Bliss Smoothie

Ingredients:

- 1 cup unsweetened almond milk
- 1/2 banana, frozen
- 1/2 teaspoon vanilla extract
- 1 tablespoon almond butter
- 1 tablespoon chia seeds
- Ice cubes

Preparation Time: 5 minutes

Method:

1. Place all ingredients in a blender.

2. Blend until smooth and creamy.
3. Pour into a glass and enjoy immediately.

With these energizing smoothie and shake recipes, you can indulge in sweet treats while nourishing your body with wholesome ingredients. Customize these recipes with your favorite fruits, nuts, and seeds to create your own signature blends. Enjoy these delicious and nutritious beverages as a satisfying snack or meal replacement any time of day.

Chapter 11: Meal Plans and Sample Menus:Week-long Low Carb Meal Plans

Achieving success on a low-carb diet requires careful planning and preparation. These week-long meal plans provide a structured approach to help you stay on track while enjoying delicious and satisfying meals.

Day 1:

- Breeakfast: Scrambled Eggs with Feta Cheese and Spinach.
  - Ingredients:
    1. 2 eggs

2. Handful of spinach
3. 1/4 cup crumbled feta cheese
4. Salt and pepper to taste
- Preparation Time: 10 minutes
- Method:
    1. Heat a non-stick skillet over medium heat.
    2. Beat the eggs and season with salt and pepper.
    3. Add spinach to the skillet and cook till wilted.
    4. Pour the whisked eggs over the spinach and cook until scrambled.

5. Sprinkle with feta cheese and serve hot.

- Lunch: Grilled Chicken Salad with Avocado and Balsamic Vinaigrette
  - Ingredients:
    1. 4 oz grilled chicken breast, sliced
    2. Mixed salad greens
    3. 1/2 avocado, sliced
    4. Balsamic vinaigrette dressing
  - Preparation Time: 15 minutes
  - Method:
    1. Arrange the salad greens on a plate.
    2. Top with sliced grilled chicken and avocado.

3. Drizzle with balsamic vinaigrette dressing.

- Dinner: Baked Salmon with Roasted Asparagus
  - Ingredients:
    1. 6 oz salmon fillet
    2. 1 bunch asparagus
    3. Olive oil
    4. Salt and pepper to taste
  - Preparation Time: 25 minutes
  - Method:
    1. Preheat the oven to 400°F (200°C).
    2. Place the salmon fillet on a baking sheet that you have already lined with parchment paper.

3. Drizzle olive oil and season with salt and pepper.
4. Trim the woody ends of the asparagus and arrange them on the baking sheet.
5. Drizzle olive oil and season.
6. Bake for 15-20 minutes until the salmon is cooked through and the asparagus is tender.

- Snack: Celery Sticks with Almond Butter
  - Ingredients:
    1. Celery sticks
    2. Almond butter

- Preparation Time: 5 minutes
- Method:
  1. Wash and trim the celery sticks.
  2. Spread almond butter on the celery sticks.
  3. Enjoy as a crunchy and satisfying snack.

Day 2:

- Breakfast: Greek Yogurt with Berries and Nuts
  - Ingredients:
    1. 1/2 cup Greek yogurt
    2. Mixed berries (e.g., strawberries, blueberries, raspberries)

3. Mixed nuts (e.g., almonds, walnuts, pecans)
- Preparation Time: 5 minutes
- Method:
    1. Spoon Greek yogurt into a bowl.
    2. Top with mixed berries and nuts.
    3. Enjoy as a creamy and satisfying breakfast option.
- Lunch: Turkey Lettuce Wraps with Hummus
    - Ingredients:
        1. Sliced turkey breast
        2. Lettuce leaves
        3. Hummus

- Preparation Time: 10 minutes
- Method:
    1. Lay lettuce leaves flat on a plate.
    2. Top each lettuce leaf with sliced turkey breast and a dollop of hummus.
    3. Roll up the lettuce leaves and enjoy as a light and flavorful lunch.
- Dinneer: Cauliflower Rice Stir-Fry with mixed vegetables and Tofu
    - Ingredients:
        1. 1 block tofu, cubed
        2. 2 cups cauliflower rice

3. Mixed vegetables (e.g., bell peppers, broccoli, carrots)
4. Soy sauce
5. Sesame oil
6. Garlic powder
7. Ginger powder

- Preparation Time: 20 minutes
- Method:
    1. Heat sesame oil in a skillet.
    2. Add cubed tofu and cook until golden brown on all sides.
    3. Push tofu to one side of the skillet and add cauliflower rice to the other side.

4. Stir-fry cauliflower rice until tender.
5. Add mixed vegetables to the skillet and cook until tender-crisp.
6. Season with some soy sauce, garlic and ginger powder.
7. Toss everything together and serve hot.

- Snack: Cheese Slices with Cucumber Slices
  - Ingredients:
    1. Cheese slices
    2. Cucumber slices
  - Preparation Time: 5 minutes
  - Method:

1. Arrange cheese slices and cucumber slices on a plate.
2. Enjoy as a simple and refreshing snack.

Day 3:

- Breakfast: Low-Carb Smoothie with Spinach, Berries, and Protein Powder
    - Ingredients:
        1. 1 cup spinach
        2. 1/2 cup mixed berries (e.g., strawberries, blueberries)
        3. 1 scoop protein powder
        4. Unsweetened almond milk

5. Ice cubes

- Preparation Time: 5 minutes
- Method:
    1. Place spinach, mixed berries, protein powder, and almond milk in a blender.
    2. Blend until smooth.
    3. Add ice cubes,blend again until you desired consistency is attained.
    4. Serve immediately.

- Lunch: Zucchini Noodles with Marinara Sauce and Grilled Shrimp
    - Ingredients:
        1. Zucchini noodles (zoodles)

2. Marinara sauce (sugar-free)

3. Grilled shrimp

- Preparation Time: 15 minutes
- Method:
    1. Spiralize zucchini to create noodles.
    2. Heat marinara sauce in a skillet.
    3. Add zucchini noodles to the skillet and cook until tender.
    4. Serve zoodles topped with grilled shrimp and marinara sauce.

- Dinner: Beef Stir-Fry with Bell Peppers and broccoli

Ingredients:

1. Thinly sliced beef
2. Broccoli florets
3. Sliced bell peppers
4. Soy sauce (low-sodium)
5. Garlic powder
6. Ginger powder
7. Sesame oil

- Preparation Time: 20 minutes
- Method:
  1. Heat sesame oil in a wok over medium-high heat.
  2. Add beef slices and cook until browned.

3. Add broccoli florets
   and sliced bell peppers
   to the skillet.
4. Stir-fry until
   vegetables are tender-
   crisp.
5. Season with soy
   sauce,ginger and garlic
   powder.
6. Serve hot.

- Snack: Hard-Boiled Eggs with
  Cherry Tomatoes
    - Ingredients:
        1. Hard-boiled eggs
        2. Cherry tomatoes
    - Preparation Time: 10
      minutes (for boiling eggs)
    - Method:

1. Peel hard-boiled eggs
   and halve them.
2. Serve with cherry
   tomatoes on the side.

Day 4:

- Breakfast: Avocado Toast on Low-
  Carb Bread
  - Ingredients:
    1. Low-carb bread slices
    2. Ripe avocado
    3. Salt and pepper
    4. Optional toppings: red
       pepper flakes, sesame
       seeds
  - Preparation Time: 5 minutes
  - Method:

1. Toast low-carb bread slices until golden brown.
2. Mash ripe avocado and spread it onto the toast.
3. Season with salt and pepper.
4. Sprinkle with optional toppings if desired.

- Lunch: Cobb Salad with Grilled Chicken, Bacon, Avocado, and Blue Cheese Dressing
  - Ingredients:
    1. Mixed salad greens
    2. Grilled chicken breast, sliced
    3. Cooked bacon, crumbled

4. Avocado, diced
5. Blue cheese dressing (sugar-free)
- Preparation Time: 15 minutes
- Method:
  1. Arrange salad greens on a plate.
  2. Top with sliced grilled chicken, crumbled bacon, diced avocado, and blue cheese dressing.

- Dinner: Grilled Steak with Roasted Brussels Sprouts
  - Ingredients:
    1. Steak (e.g., ribeye, sirloin)
    2. Brussels sprouts

3. Olive oil

4. Salt and pepper

- Preparation Time: 25 minutes
- Method:

    1. Preheat grill to medium-high heat.

    2. Rub steak with olive oil, salt, and pepper.

    3. Grill steak to desired doneness.

    4. Trim Brussels sprouts and halve them.

    5. Toss Brussels sprouts with some salt, olive oil, and pepper.

    6. Roast in the oven until crispy and golden brown.

- Snack: Almonds and String Cheese
  - Ingredients:
    1. Almonds
    2. String cheese
  - Preparation Time: None
  - Method:
    1. Enjoy a handful of almonds with string cheese for a quick and satisfying snack.

Day 5:

- Breakfast: Chia Seed Pudding with Coconut Milk and Berries
  - Ingredients:
    1. 2 tablespoons chia seeds

2. 1/2 cup unsweetened coconut milk
3. Mixed berries
4. Optional: unsweetened shredded coconut

- Preparation Time: 5 minutes (plus chilling time)
- Method:
    1. In a bowl, mix chia seeds and coconut milk. Let it sit for a few minutes, then stir again.
    2. Cover and refrigerate for at least 2 hours or overnight, until it reaches a pudding-like consistency.

3. Serve topped with mixed berries and shredded coconut if desired.
- Lunch: Tuna Salad Lettuce Wraps with Cucumber and Tomato
  - Ingredients:
    1. Canned tuna, drained
    2. Mayonnaise (sugar-free)
    3. Diced celery
    4. Lettuce leaves
    5. Sliced cucumber
    6. Sliced tomato
  - Preparation Time: 10 minutes
  - Method:

1. In a bowl, mix canned tuna with mayonnaise and diced celery.
2. Spoon the tuna salad onto lettuce leaves.
3. Top with sliced cucumber and tomato.
4. Roll up the lettuce leaves and enjoy.

- Dinner: Spaghetti Squash with Pesto and Grilled Chicken
  - Ingredients:
    1. Spaghetti squash
    2. Pesto sauce (sugar-free)
    3. Grilled chicken breast, sliced
    4. Fresh basil leaves

5. Optional: grated Parmesan cheese

- Preparation Time: 45 minutes
- Method:
    1. Preheat oven to 400°F (200°C).
    2. Then,Cut the spaghetti squash in half i.e lengthwise and remove it's seeds.
    3. Place the squash halves, which you have cut side down, on a baking sheet.
    4. Bake for 30-40 minutes until tender.
    5. Scrape the flesh of the squash with a fork to

create "spaghetti" strands.

6. Toss spaghetti squash with pesto sauce and top with grilled chicken.

7. Garnish with fresh basil leaves, grated Parmesan cheese if you desire.

- Snack: Greek Yogurt with Sliced Almonds
  - Ingredients:
    1. Greek yogurt
    2. Sliced almonds
  - Preparation Time: 5 minutes
  - Method:
    1. Spoon Greek yogurt into a bowl.

2. Top with sliced
   almonds for a crunchy
   and protein-rich snack.

Day 6:

- Breakfast: Veggie Omelette with
  Mushrooms, Onions, and Bell
  Peppers
  - Ingredients:
    1. Eggs
    2. Sliced mushrooms
    3. Diced onions
    4. Sliced bell peppers
    5. Olive oil
    6. Salt and pepper
  - Preparation Time: 10
    minutes
  - Method:

1. Heat olive oil in a skillet over medium heat.
2. Add sliced mushrooms, diced onions, and sliced bell peppers to the skillet. Cook until vegetables are tender.
3. Beat the eggs and season with salt and pepper.
4. Pour eggs over the cooked vegetables in the skillet.
5. Cook until the omelette is set and golden brown on the bottom.

6. Fold the omelette in half and serve hot.
- Lunch: Egg Salad Stuffed Tomatoes
    - Ingredients:
        1. Hard-boiled eggs, chopped
        2. Mayonnaise (sugar-free)
        3. Dijon mustard
        4. Salt and pepper
        5. Large tomatoes
        6. Fresh parsley, chopped (optional)
    - Preparation Time: 15 minutes
    - Method:
        1. In a bowl, mix chopped hard-boiled

eggs with mayonnaise, Dijon mustard, salt, and pepper.

2. Slice the tops off the tomatoes and scoop out the seeds to create a hollow cavity.

3. Stuff each tomato with the egg salad mixture.

4. Garnish with chopped parsley if desired.

- Dinner: Baked Cod with Steamed Broccoli
    - Ingredients:
        1. Cod fillets
        2. Lemon juice
        3. Garlic powder
        4. Paprika
        5. Salt and pepper

6. Broccoli florets
- Preparation Time: 20 minutes
- Method:
  1. Preheat oven to 400°F (200°C).
  2. Then place the cod fillets on a baking sheet that you've lined with parchment paper.
  3. Drizzle with lemon juice and season with garlic powder, paprika, salt, and pepper.
  4. Bake for about 12-15 minutes until the fish flakes easily with a fork.

5. Steam broccoli florets until tender.

6. Serve baked cod with steamed broccoli on the side.

- Snack: Cottage Cheese with Pineapple Chunks
    - Ingredients:
        1. Cottage cheese
        2. Pineapple chunks
    - Preparation Time: 5 minutes
    - Method:
        1. Spoon cottage cheese into a bowl.
        2. Top with pineapple chunks for a sweet and creamy snack.

Day 7:

- Breakfast: Breakfast Burrito Bowl with Scrambled Eggs, Avocado, and Salsa
  - Ingredients:
    1. Scrambled eggs
    2. Avocado slices
    3. Salsa (sugar-free)
    4. Optional toppings: diced bell peppers, chopped onions, shredded cheese
  - Preparation Time: 10 minutes
  - Method:
    1. Arrange scrambled eggs in a bowl.
    2. Top with avocado slices, salsa, and any desired toppings.

- Lunch: Caprese Salad with Fresh Mozzarella, Tomatoes, and Basil
    - Ingredients:
        1. Fresh mozzarella cheese, sliced
        2. Ripe tomatoes, sliced
        3. Fresh basil leaves
        4. Balsamic glaze (sugar-free)
        5. Olive oil
        6. Salt and pepper
    - Preparation Time: 10 minutes
    - Method:
        1. Arrange slices of fresh mozzarella cheese and ripe tomatoes on a plate.

2. Top with fresh basil leaves.
3. Drizzle with balsamic glaze and olive oil.
4. Season with salt and pepper to taste.

- Dinner: Turkey Meatballs with Zucchini Noodles and Marinara Sauce
    - Ingredients:
        1. Ground turkey
        2. Almond flour
        3. Egg
        4. Garlic powder
        5. Dried oregano
        6. Zucchini noodles (zoodles)
        7. Marinara sauce (sugar-free)

- Preparation Time: 30 minutes
- Method:
    1. In a bowl, mix ground turkey with almond flour, egg, garlic powder, and dried oregano.
    2. Roll the mixture into meatballs and place on a baking sheet.
    3. Bake meatballs in the oven at 375°F (190°C) for 20-25 minutes until cooked through.
    4. Heat marinara sauce in a skillet.

5. Add zucchini noodles to the skillet and cook until tender.

6. Serve the turkey meatballs on top of the zucchini noodles and marinara sauce.

- Snack: Veggie Sticks with Guacamole
  - Ingredients:
    1. Assorted vegetable sticks (e.g., carrots, celery, bell peppers)
    2. Guacamole
  - Preparation Time: 10 minutes
  - Method:
    1. Wash and cut assorted vegetables into sticks.

2. Serve with guacamole
   for dipping.

Conclusion

Congratulations on completing your journey through the world of low-carb living and anti-inflammatory nutrition! As you reflect on the knowledge gained and the delicious recipes discovered, it's important to consider the long-term strategies that will support your health and wellness goals for years to come.

Embracing Your Low Carb Lifestyle

Embracing a low-carb lifestyle is not just about temporary dietary changes; it's about adopting a sustainable approach to eating that nourishes your body, supports your health goals, and enhances your overall well-being. By prioritizing whole, nutrient-dense foods and minimizing processed carbohydrates, you're providing your body with the fuel it needs to thrive.

Long-Term Strategies for Health and Wellness

As you continue on your low-carb journey, here are some long-term strategies to keep in mind:

- Consistency is Key: Stay consistent with your dietary choices and lifestyle habits. Remember that sustainable progress is achieved through steady, persistent effort over time.
- Listen to Your Body: Pay attention to how different foods make you

feel and adjust your dietary choices accordingly. Your body is unique, and its needs may change over time.

- Practice Balance: Strive for balance in your diet by incorporating a variety of nutrient-rich foods from all food groups. This ensures that you're meeting your nutritional needs while enjoying a diverse and satisfying diet.

- Stay Active: Regular physical activity is an essential component of a healthy lifestyle. Find activities you enjoy and do them everyday.

- Prioritize Self-Care: Take time to prioritize self-care and stress management. Engage in activities that help you relax, unwind, and recharge, such as meditation, yoga, or spending time in nature.

- Seek Support: Surround yourself with a supportive community of friends, family, or like-minded individuals who share your health goals.

By incorporating these long-term strategies into your lifestyle, you can continue to reap the benefits of your low-carb journey for years to come. Remember that health and wellness are lifelong pursuits, and each day presents an opportunity to nourish your body, mind, and spirit.

As you embark on the next phase of your journey, remember the principles you've learned and the delicious recipes you've discovered. With dedication, mindfulness, and a commitment to self-care, you can create a life filled with health, vitality, and abundance.

Thank you for joining us on this journey, and may your low-carb lifestyle be a source of joy, fulfillment, and well-being for years to come. Here's to your health and happiness!

MEAL PLANNER! MEAL PLANNER! MEAL PLANNER !!

Days	B. Fast	Lunch	Dinner
Mon			
Tue			
Wed			
Thu			

Friday			
Sat			
Sun			

Days	B. Fast	Lunch	Dinner
Mon			
Tue			
Wed			

Thu			
Friday			
Sat			
Sun			

Days	B. Fast	Lunch	Dinner
Mon			
Tue			

Wed			
Thu			
Friday			
Sat			

Sun			

Days	B. Fast	Lunch	Dinner

Mon			
Tue			
Wed			
Thu			
Friday			

Sat			
Sun			

Days	B. Fast	Lunch	Dinner
Mon			
Tue			
Wed			
Thu			

Friday			
Sat			
Sun			

Days	B. Fast	Lunch	Dinner
Mon			
Tue			
Wed			

Thu			
Friday			
Sat			
Sun			

Days	B. Fast	Lunch	Dinner
Mon			
Tue			

Wed			
Thu			
Friday			
Sat			

Days	B. Fast	Lunch	Dinner
Sun			

Mon			
Tue			
Wed			
Thu			
Friday			

Sat			
Sun			

Happy Cooking !!!!

Made in United States
Troutdale, OR
12/23/2024

27196083R00216